Becoming Who God Says I Am

IDENTITY

Becoming Who God Says I Am
IDENTITY

By Ralph Ennis, Judy Gomoll, Dennis Stokes, and Christine Weddle

NAVPRESS

BE TRANSFORMED

BE TRANSFORMED

NavPress is the publishing ministry of The Navigators, an international Christian organization and leader in personal spiritual development. NavPress is committed to helping people grow spiritually and enjoy lives of meaning and hope through personal and group resources that are biblically rooted, culturally relevant, and highly practical.

For a free catalog go to www.NavPress.com
or call 1.800.366.7788 in the United States or 1.800.839.4769 in Canada.

ISBN-13: 978-1-60006-259-9
ISBN-10: 1-60006-259-8

Cover design by The DesignWorks Group, Jason Gabbert, www.thedesignworksgroup.com

Content Development Team: Ralph Ennis, Judy Gomoll, Dennis Stokes, and Christine Weddle

Some of the anecdotal illustrations in this book are true to life and are included with the permission of the persons involved. All other illustrations are composites of real situations, and any resemblance to people living or dead is coincidental.

Printed in China

1 2 3 4 5 6 7 8 / 12 11 10 09 08

CONTENTS

INTRODUCTION

The whole focus of this study is on identity — discovering God's perspective on who we really are (and are not) and learning to live authentically out of that identity. This study isn't about unhealthy, self-absorbed introspection. Rather it's about one critical piece of Jesus' greatest commandment to "love the Lord your God" and to "love your neighbor as yourself" (Mark 12:30-31). "As [you love] yourself." No matter how hard we try, we cannot grow in loving God or loving others unless we are also growing in loving ourselves. Of course the journey of knowing, accepting, and loving yourself as you truly are in Christ will take every day of your life for the rest of your life. But there are some important signs, experiences, and decision points along the way that you don't want to miss.

You've probably been on the "Who am I?" journey for quite a while. Your current sense of identity is most likely a mixture of some truths and some half-truths and a few lies, of dreams and disillusionments, of wonders and wounds. So how can you sort out who you really are, much less grow to really accept and love who you are? The Bible describes our identity as something imparted to us by our Creator — not something we patch together for ourselves. It combines our one-of-a-kind distinctiveness with characteristics of God's image embedded in all humans — because all humans are created in His image. There is a vital connection between God's true identity and our true identity as human persons. If we want to find out what's true and good about us, we begin by discovering what's true and good about God and how He originally made us. Any honest discussion of what's good about us has to acknowledge what's also really bad about us, and all humanity. You'll find that embedded in every chapter, too. But ultimately we hope these studies will release you to love yourself and live out of who God says you are as you experience God's redemption — so that you can better experience loving God and others.

CHAPTER FLOW

Think of your time spent in each chapter as a mini journey — an exploratory trip into a significant topic on your way toward authentic spiritual transformation through Jesus.

Most chapters in each module have the following sections where you will "pause" your heart and mind along the way.

A SHORT STORY

Each is based on real-life experiences.

PAUSE 1: EXPLORING WHAT GOD SAYS

This section encourages you to look at the Bible to see what God has said. We'll print out most of the verses for you, from a variety of Bible translations. But nothing beats reading your own Bible to make you comfortable in God's Word. You'll be reading the *New International Version* (NIV), unless we say otherwise. Sometimes we use The Message (MSG), *The New Living Translation* (NLT), *The Living Bible* (TLB), or the *Amplified Bible* (AMP). As you move from chapter to chapter, you will gradually try different approaches to studying, processing, and applying these passages.

PAUSE 2: EXPLORING YOUR REALITY

Our information-driven society makes it easy to walk away from profound truth without considering what it really says about us. This section helps you identify where you are in terms of the topic, and how you got there. You will also explore what it might take for you to become more like Jesus.

PAUSE 3: COMING ALIVE TO GOD AND OTHERS

Our "What's-in-it-for-me?" culture often promotes self-centeredness and shallowness in our relationships. This section will help you examine biblical principles for knowing and relating to God and others with authenticity, honesty, humility, and love.

PAUSE 4: JOURNEYING FORWARD

Being connected with Jesus as your default lifestyle means learning to trust Him with what's true about you — all the way, every day. This section invites you to process and write out what you are learning as you live in Him, as well as what you're doing about what you are learning. We strongly encourage you to memorize the key verse provided for each chapter as a way of building this vital spiritual discipline into your journey.

DIGGING DEEPER

Like the photo album you make after a trip, in this optional section you can pause to recap and process the highlights of your experience so far. We'll give you a few "extras" if you want to explore and experience the topic of the chapter more deeply.

IMAGES

In each chapter we've included pictures and artwork to help you reflect on the topics. They are there to stimulate your imagination and heart when words fall short. Take time to gaze at the images and place yourself within these visual stories. If a photo disturbs you, that's okay; try to figure out why.

YOUR JOURNEY THROUGH EACH CHAPTER

For each chapter, expect to devote about an hour to personal preparation — more if you choose to do the optional "Digging Deeper" section. So pace yourself. You might try working a little at a time on a chapter — say, one section a day or twenty minutes a day or take a longer time of concentrated reflection. Find a rhythm that fits you best. Your group may want to consider discussing one chapter per session or dividing up the chapter and discussing it in two sessions.

FOR GROUP LEADERS

We've provided a leader's guide that can be downloaded at www.NavPress.com. Search for the ISBN or book title.

GUIDELINES FOR SMALL GROUPS

1. Confidentiality: Do not repeat anything said or heard inside the group to anyone outside the group. Refraining from gossip builds trust.

2. Safety: Respect each other's boundaries. Also accept each other's perceived realities without needing to comment or "fix" how someone feels or sees things at the moment. Nobody should feel forced to share anything that they prefer to keep private. Providing each other space and supportive care will promote safety.

3. "I" Statements: Be yourself; take off your masks. Share information only about yourself — not "we, they, or us."

4. Interference: Avoid giving advice, talking while someone else is sharing, or subtly competing by saying, "I'm just like you" or by sharing a similar story. Instead, listen attentively, learn from each other's life experiences, and offer brief and affirming feedback.

5. Individuality: Accept and enjoy the diversity in your group, including being at very different places on your spiritual journeys. Allow everyone (but don't force anyone) to discover areas of need or brokenness. Avoid probing or intrusive questioning, as well as tampering with or elaborating on each other's personal sharing.

6. Emotional Sharing: Expect and allow each other to experience a full range of emotions, even if this makes you uncomfortable. This might include crying, raising their voice, or being silent. When this happens, avoid interrupting, communicating that another's feelings are unacceptable or "bad." And don't touch or hug without permission. Allow for times of quiet in your group because silence can be one of the most powerful healing environments.

7. Roadblocks and Obstacles: It is important to allow people to process their thoughts and feelings without needing to come to clear resolution. It is also normal to experience obstacles and setbacks. Remember that being stuck can be a catalyst for members to move forward. Trust the process!

8. Holy Spirit: Only God can perform the healing and growth needed in our hearts. The purpose of the group is to provide a place where the support, love, and acceptance of God can be modeled and felt and where the truth of God can be discovered and embraced.

9. Personal Responsibility: Recognize that true life change can occur only with God's help as we yield to His leading. The group can provide accountability through prayer and support.

10. Group Limits: Don't expect your group to provide therapy, counseling, or other in-depth one-to-one support for members. Know when to refer each other to someone outside your group who is better equipped to help.

BENEFITS OF HEALTHY GROUP PROCESS

1. A safe place to share vulnerably and honestly.
2. New relationships.
3. An opportunity to be listened to in an accepting and grace-filled environment.
4. A forum for embracing truth, gaining perspective, and growing spiritually at your own pace.

FOR GROUP DISCUSSION: After reading these guidelines together, discuss these questions in the group:

Knowing myself, here are several practical things I will do to help make our group a safe place:

-
-
-

In a small group these specific things can make me feel unsafe:

-
-
-

Take time to pray together before you begin this journey.

CHAPTER 1
GOD'S ESSENCE: WHAT'S GOOD ABOUT HIM?

About the only time Jesse ever heard his mother mention God was before a meal: "God is great, God is good, and we thank Him for our food . . ." Actually, it was more of a chant than a prayer. So, if God was so good, why was He so conspicuously unmentioned and irrelevant the rest of the time?

For years, Jesse's infrequent reflections on God were mostly for the sake of argument or philosophical peace. But then his best friend in high school died in a tragic accident. Jesse began struggling with thoughts about God. For months stretching into years, he couldn't square the mealtime-blessing image of this "great and good God" with such senseless pain. Unable to resolve the question of whether God was good or not, he just blocked it from his mind. Not thinking about God at all was less painful than wrestling with the goodness of God in the face of his anger and loneliness.

Jesse was in his late twenties before he finally connected the numbness of his heart to that day he turned away from struggling with the goodness of God and just gave up. He was getting engaged and hoping to be a dad someday. That's what made him start wondering if, maybe, God really could be good after all. He wondered if God might even be good enough to restore his numb heart to life.

PAUSE 1_EXPLORING WHAT GOD SAYS

Let's explore God's character and what it has to do with our identity.

> *GENESIS 1:26-27,31. God said, Let Us [Father, Son, and Holy Spirit] make mankind in Our image, after Our likeness, and let them have complete authority over the fish of the sea, the birds of the air, the [tame] beasts, and over all of the earth, and over everything that creeps upon the earth. So God created man in His own image, in the image and likeness of God He cre-ated him; male and female He created them. . . . And God saw everything that He had made, and behold, it was very good (suitable, pleasant) and He approved it completely.* (AMP)

God, the Creator of the entire universe, chose to make us human beings (and only us human beings) in His image. We reflect the very likeness of God. What do you think this means?

What do you think was "very good" (verse 31) about our original design?

The creation account in Genesis implies that if we want to find out what's true and good about us, we begin by discovering what's true and good about God. Why? Because God designed us to be like Him in some very important ways.

> *God the Creator is transcendent, mysterious, and inscrutable, beyond the range of any imagining or philosophical guesswork of which we are capable; and hence a summons to us to humble ourselves, to listen and learn of Him, and to let Him teach us what He is like and how we should think of Him.*
>
> — J. I. PACKER, *KNOWING GOD*

Throughout this study we'll use the illustration of light passing through a prism to depict what is so dazzling about God. A prism is a piece of crystal that takes rays of invisible light, refracts them, and reveals a rainbow of different colors contained in that light. Similarly,

God is invisible to human beings. If God hadn't chosen to reveal Himself, we wouldn't have a clue what He's really like. He longs for us to know Him as He truly is. He revealed many things about Himself to us through the "prisms" of His created world, the Scriptures, His Son Jesus, our consciences, and history. These are just some of the ways God shows us His "true colors," so to speak.

PSALM 145:1-3 gives us a panoramic view of what's good about God. Study these verses from your Bible for words or phrases that describe God. Write those words or phrases on the prism illustration below.

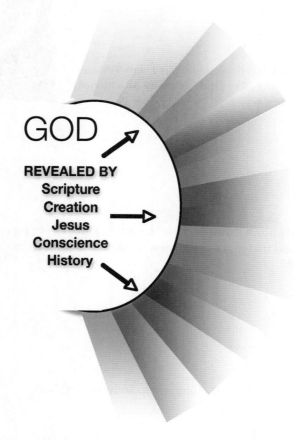

NOTE: A prism doesn't "reveal" all of the rays contained in light, like ultraviolet or infrared rays. Similarly, there is much more about God revealed elsewhere in Scripture, through creation, and through the Person of Jesus — as well as things about God we'll never see on this earth (see Deuteronomy 29:29).

PAUSE 2_EXPLORING YOUR REALITY

We live in a very pluralistic world with too many options to count. Culture says you can have your choice of gods, too. Besides the God of the Bible, what other gods are out there that people believe in? How do they differ from God (Father, Son, and Holy Spirit)?

Sometimes people like God, but they also dislike Him. Ask several people you know if they like God, and why or why not. Summarize their responses here.

You can be sure that God knows if you find Him unlikable sometimes; He isn't surprised. Are there things about God that make you uncomfortable or confused or that you just don't like? Explain.

Do you think you'd feel any differently if you got to know Him better?

Where do you think your concept of God came from? List several possible influences.

What influence do you think your view of your earthly father (even if you never knew him) might have had on your view of your heavenly Father? Explain.

> EXAMPLE: My dad worked all the time and hardly ever relaxed or played. So I viewed God as a no-nonsense God, always practical and taking care of basic needs and essentials. I didn't think He was interested in my wild, impractical dreams or would ever just splurge on me.

What about you?

The early conception of God is almost invariably founded upon the child's idea of his father.
— J. B. PHILLIPS, *YOUR GOD IS TOO SMALL*

The greatest obstacle to realizing our dreams is the false self's hatred of mystery. That's a problem, you see, because mystery is essential to adventure. More than that, mystery is the heart of the universe and the God who made it.
— JOHN ELDREDGE, *WILD AT HEART*

You are invited to step into the mystery of God. How does this invitation encourage you toward a life of adventure with Him?

PAUſE 3_COMING ALIVE TO GOD AND OTHERſ

Behind the "Who am I?" question is the even bigger "Who is God?" question. In Pause 1 you took a panoramic view of God's character. Now you're going to zoom in on some of God's attributes. As you read:

1. Mark up the key words and phrases about God in these verses with underlining or highlighting.
2. In the margins, summarize what you have observed about who God is and what He's like.
3. HEADS UP! This Pause is packed with Scripture verses — some of the most awesome verses in the Bible, because they describe our God. Don't feel compelled to do all twelve attributes if your time is short. Do as many as it takes to understand that the one and only God has revealed His character to us in these ways. Just enjoy getting to know Him more accurately and intimately.

Explain and Expand:

God used His great power to create the whole universe and everything in it.

1. GOD IS ALL POWERFUL

JEREMIAH 10:12-13. But God made the earth by his power; he founded the world by his wisdom and stretched out the heavens by his understanding. When he thunders, the waters in the heavens roar; he makes clouds rise from the ends of the earth. He sends lightning with the rain and brings out the wind from his storehouses.

Absolutely nothing is too hard for God to do.

JEREMIAH 32:17-19. Ah, Sovereign LORD, you have made the heavens and the earth by your great power and outstretched arm. Nothing is too hard for you. . . . O great and powerful God, whose name is the LORD Almighty, great are your purposes and mighty are your deeds.

Explain and Expand:

2. GOD IS ETERNAL AND IS PRESENT EVERYWHERE

PSALM 90:1-2.
Lord, through all the generations
*   you have been our home!*
Before the mountains were born,
*   before you gave birth to the earth and the world,*
*   from beginning to end, you are God. (NLT)*

PSALM 139:7-10.
Where can I go from your Spirit?
Where can I flee from your presence?
If I go up to the heavens, you are there;
if I make my bed in the depths, you are there.
If I rise on the wings of the dawn,
if I settle on the far side of the sea,
even there your hand will guide me,
your right hand will hold me fast.

REVELATION 1:8.
"I am the Alpha and the Omega — the beginning and the end,"
says the Lord God. "I am the one who is, who always was, and
who is still to come, the Almighty One." (NLT)

The Scriptures teach that God is infinite. This means that His being knows no limits. Therefore there can be no limit to His presence; He is omnipresent. Because He is infinite, He surrounds the finite creation and contains it. There is no place beyond Him for anything to be. God is our environment as the sea is to the fish and the air to the bird. "God is over all things," wrote Hildebert of Lavardin, "under all things; outside all; within but not enclosed; without but not excluded; above but not raised up; below but not depressed; wholly above, presiding; wholly beneath, sustaining; wholly within, filling."

— A. W. TOZER, *THE KNOWLEDGE OF THE HOLY*

3. GOD IS TRIUNE (three Persons in One)

Explain and Expand:

GENESIS 1:26. Then God said, "Let us make man in our image, in our likeness."

DEUTERONOMY 6:4. Hear, O Israel: The LORD our God, the LORD is one.

JOHN 14:16-17,31. And I [Jesus] will ask the Father, and he will give you another Counselor to be with you forever — the Spirit of truth. The world cannot accept him, because it neither sees him nor knows him. But you know him, for he lives with you and will be in you. . . . The world must learn that I love the Father.

4. GOD IS THE INDEPENDENT CREATOR

Explain and Expand:

NEHEMIAH 9:6. You alone are the LORD. You made the heavens, even the highest heavens, and all their starry host, the earth and all that is on it, the seas and all that is in them. You give life to everything, and the multitudes of heaven worship you.

COLOSSIANS 1:15-16. He [Jesus] is the image of the invisible God, the firstborn over all creation. For by him all things were created: things in heaven and on earth, visible and invisible, whether thrones or powers or rulers or authorities; all things were created by him and for him.

Explain and Expand:

5. GOD IS MORALLY GOOD

PSALM 25:8. The Lord is good and does what is right; he shows the proper path to those who go astray. (NLT)

ROMANS 2:4. Or do you show contempt for the riches of his kindness, tolerance and patience, not realizing that God's kindness leads you toward repentance?

REVELATION 15:4. Who will not fear you, O Lord, and bring glory to your name? For you alone are holy. All nations will come and worship before you, for your righteous acts have been revealed.

Explain and Expand:

6. GOD IS TRUE AND JUST

DEUTERONOMY 32:4. He is the Rock, his works are perfect, and all his ways are just. A faithful God who does no wrong, upright and just is he.

ROMANS 3:4. Even if everyone else is a liar, God is true. As the Scriptures say about him, "You will be proved right in what you say, and you will win your case in court." (NLT)

REVELATION 15:3. Great and marvelous are your deeds, Lord God Almighty. Just and true are your ways, King of the ages.

Explain and Expand:

7. GOD IS LOVE

NEHEMIAH 9:17. But you are a forgiving God, gracious and compassionate, slow to anger and abounding in love. Therefore you did not desert them.

JEREMIAH 31:3. The Lord appeared to us in the past, saying: "I have loved you with an everlasting love; I have drawn you with loving-kindness."

1 JOHN 3:1. How great is the love the Father has lavished on us, that we should be called children of God!

1 JOHN 4:8,19. Whoever does not love does not know God, because God is love. . . . We love because he first loved us.

God wants us to adore Him, dance with Him, eat, drink, and sing with Him in the experience of His awesome, glorious love. The mystery of His desire is that an eternal, infinite, holy, and utterly self-fulfilling Being wants us — and he is willing to go to any lengths whatsoever to disrupt, arouse, and stop us from pursuing any lover other than Himself. Through His unfathomable desire for us and His paradoxical methods of wooing us, He reveals His goodness.
— DR. DAN B. ALLENDER & DR. TREMPER LONGMAN III, *THE CRY OF THE SOUL*

8. GOD IS JEALOUS

EXODUS 34:14. Do not worship any other god, for the LORD, whose name is Jealous, is a jealous God.

2 CORINTHIANS 11:2. I [Paul] am jealous for you with a godly jealousy. I promised you to one husband, to Christ, so that I might present you as a pure virgin to him.

Explain and Expand:

Is fiercely protective of His people whom He cherishes.

God is a romantic at heart, and he has his own bride to fight for. He is a jealous lover, and his jealousy is for the hearts of his people and for their freedom.
— JOHN ELDREDGE, *WILD AT HEART*

9. GOD IS GLORIOUS AND BEAUTIFUL

Explain and Expand:

EXODUS 15:11. Who is like you among the gods, O LORD — glorious in holiness, awesome in splendor, performing great wonders? (NLT)

PSALM 29:2. Give unto the LORD the glory due to His name; worship the LORD in the beauty of holiness. (NKJV)

PSALM 72:19. Praise be to his glorious name forever; may the whole earth be filled with his glory. Amen and Amen.

CONSIDER THIS: Not only is God all of these things — ever-present, all-powerful, loving, beautiful, etc. — but He will always be these things and will never change. And this is only a small part of who God is. We simply can't fathom all His mysteries, or probe the limits of His nature. How does this constancy and depth of God affect you?

God has revealed many other attributes about Himself that we didn't mention above. For instance, He is also Spirit, all-knowing, unchanging, purposeful, and incomprehensible. Are there any other attributes of God that are especially meaningful or perplexing to you? Add them to the following prism illustration.

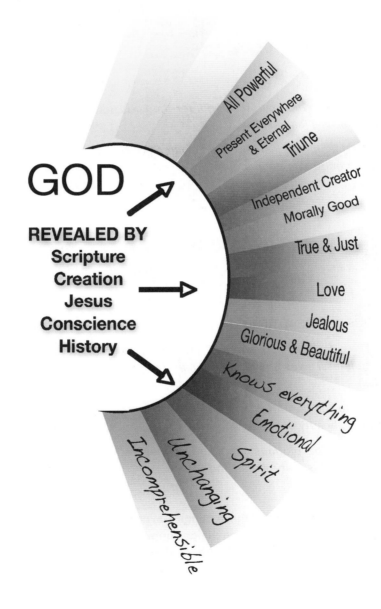

To what extent do you think you ever really know a God like this?

Think about your view of God. Is He safe? Does your God need to be safe? What if He is wild?

METAPHOR: Looking at God's attributes is like gazing at a sparkling diamond or a many-faceted gemstone. Create your own metaphor:

Looking at God is like . . .

What comes into our minds when we think about God is the most important thing about us. The most portentous fact about any man is not what he at a given time may do, but what he in his deep heart conceives God to be like. We tend by a secret law of the soul to move toward our mental image of God. . . . That our idea of God corresponds as nearly as possible to the true being of God is of immense importance to us.
— A. W. TOZER, *THE KNOWLEDGE OF THE HOLY*

If Tozer is right, and we tend to "move toward our mental image of God," where is your current view of God likely to take you?

Consider Tozer's words again. Has this study uncovered anything "unworthy" about the way you view God? If so, describe it.

What will it take for you to "let Him be the God in [your mind] that He is in His universe"?

AUTHENTICITY PAUSE:

"God wishes to be seen, and he wishes to be sought, and he wishes to be expected, and he wishes to be trusted."
— JULIAN OF NORWICH, QUOTED BY DALLAS WILLARD, *THE DIVINE CONSPIRACY*

Take some time in prayer to consider who God is and what He wishes. Focus this time on talking to God about who He really is and about your desire to experience Him deeply.

If there are things you don't like about God, this is a good time to talk with Him about that, too.

PAUSE 4_JOURNEYING FORWARD

It's your life . . . it's your journey. So that means it's up to you how you respond to the ideas in this chapter. Pause 4 in every chapter will be like this one — completely open-ended to invite you to zero in on whatever specifically touched you most. Or whatever disturbed you the most.

> EPHESIANS 4:1. I . . . beg you to lead a life worthy of your calling, for you have been called by God. (NLT)

Whatever that is, grab on to it — don't gloss over it! During this final Pause, revisit that verse and respond to one or more of the reflective questions.

At the end of every chapter we'll invite you to select one verse or passage that you read, studied, listened to, or memorized during the week that was meaningful to you. Begin by copying the verse and its reference below, so you'll be able to find it later.

We live in a world of images that deeply influence how we look at life. Choose a picture from this chapter that is meaningful or disturbing to you, and briefly explain why.

Then, you'll be invited to select one or more of these reflective questions and journal your response. The point is not to answer all of the questions, but to help focus your reflection on what God is saying to you. Most chapters have a final journal page to give you space to write. From this study is there some . . .

PROMISE from God for me to embrace?

ACTION to take?

THOUGHT about God or life to consider?

THANKFULNESS to offer?

EMOTION to express in an honest and godly way?

RELATIONSHIP to build up or reconcile?

NEED to meet?

SINFUL action or motive to confess and forsake?

JOURNAL

Think of the journal page as part of your spiritual fitness routine. Your spirit, heart, and mind have just finished some vigorous exercise. This is the cool-down phase. Not to be hurried. We suggest two things:

1. Journal on any of the preceding reflective questions.
2. Memorize and meditate on the Scripture memory verse below.

If at all possible, don't leave your study time without capturing in writing the most important things God revealed to you.

SUGGESTED MEMORY VERSE:

GOD'S GOODNESS — PSALM 34:8

Taste and see that the Lord is good; blessed is the man who takes refuge in him.

Last, we'll suggest a key verse on the chapter's topic for you to memorize. If a different verse touched you more, feel free to substitute it. Taking 5–10 minutes right after completing the chapter study to memorize the verse may help anchor what you've learned in your heart and mind. After you have memorized the verse, check your accuracy. Try to write the verse from memory in the space below.

CHAPTER 2
CREATED IN GOD'S IMAGE: WHAT'S POSITIVE ABOUT ME?

Anastasia couldn't figure it out. The "Who am I?" question confronted her around every corner of life. And there were so many other voices trying to impose their answers on her. Who she really was kept getting drowned out by who others told her she was.

The voice of her mother rang loudest: "You're a failure. Nothing you do will ever be good enough." The voice of her friends said, "You're okay, but a little weird."

Her boyfriend's voice seemed to be muffled and confused by his own search for who he was.

And the voice of God? Well, she hadn't considered listening to what He had to say about who she is.

WHY DOES IDENTITY MATTER ANYWAY?

From birth, human beings are on a quest to discover who they are. First we look to our families to help us define our role, to test our talents and our limits, and to give us a sense of our value. Then we begin to absorb impressions from a wider world of peers, teachers, employers, hobbies, and faith to further discover ourselves.

Whatever our conclusion, how we answer the basic question, "Who am I?" will shape our relationships with others and our responses to life. For example, if I think of myself as a cosmic accident, I may discount my value; perhaps I will have no sense of belonging in a group of other "accidents" like myself and I'll just tune them out. Since my identity doesn't feel essential to the fabric of life, then talents and abilities may be unexplored and undeveloped. Opportunities may slip by; consequences may matter little, or they may terrify me.

On the other hand, what if I believe a Creator designed me with a unique personality?

What if I believe that He designed me with specific skills, abilities, and talents? That He called me for a purpose that's fulfilling and significant, that He adopted me into a family along with other equals? All of a sudden everyday life would be shot through with meaning and purpose. It would change everything.

PAUSE 1_EXPLORING WHAT GOD SAYS

To help us understand how we reflect God, we have to understand the word "image." The Hebrew word for "image" is "tselem," meaning shade or phantom. It suggests that we each bear a phantom reflection of our Creator. The word "likeness" ("demuwth" in Hebrew) tells us that the divine image we bear corresponds to the original pattern.
— JONATHAN S. CAMPBELL WITH JENNIFER CAMPBELL, *THE WAY OF JESUS*

Meditate again on these verses that define our identity at creation.

GENESIS 1:26-27,31. Then God said, "Let us make human beings in our image, to be like us. They will reign over the fish in the sea, the birds in the sky, the livestock, all the wild animals on the earth, and the small animals that scurry along the ground." So God created human beings in his own image. In the image of God he created them; male and female he created them. . . . Then God looked over all he had made, and he saw that it was very good! (NLT)

What do you think it means to be made in God's own image or patterned after God Himself?

To understand who we are, we must know more about who God is. Here's why: If God created us, and He created us in His image, then who God is defines who we are in some important ways. Of course, there are also many ways that we are not like God since finite, imperfect beings can't possibly be infinite or perfect. We're not exact replicas: whereas God is limitless, we have limits in each area. On top of the limits of being finite, there is also the devastation that sin does to our souls and in the world. We'll explore that in chapters 3 and 4. But regardless of all our imperfections, every person has dignity because every person bears God's image.

Let's try unpacking what it means that all people — not just those we are comfortable with — are created in God's image. We'll revisit the same nine attributes of God that we studied in chapter 1. But this time, after reading and marking the following verses provided, try to answer two questions:

- How do we humans reflect God positively in our nature and design?
- How are we limited in this reflection?

HEADS UP: God is infinite, so there is nothing comprehensive about this list of His attributes. Feel free to select some of the following attributes — rather than trying to do them all.

1. GOD IS ALL POWERFUL . . . and because we're created in His image, we:

[Example] We have been given the capacity to pour our energy and creative powers into significant work and contributions.

HEBREWS 2:7-8. Then you [God] put them [man and woman] in charge of your entire handcrafted world. When God put them in charge of everything, nothing was excluded. But we don't see it yet, don't see everything under human jurisdiction. (MSG)

JAMES 4:13-15. Now listen, you who say, "Today or tomorrow we will go to this or that city, spend a year there, carry on business and make money." Why, you do not even know what will happen tomorrow. What is your life? You are a mist that appears for a little while and then vanishes. Instead, you ought to say, "If it is the Lord's will, we will live and do this or that."

We are made like God in our creative powers because we are to be like God in ruling the earth. The image implies a capacity, and the capacity assumes the creative legacy we shall carry on. Our original design was for a life of creative rule, to share in the overall care and development of God's creation.

— JOHN ELDREDGE, THE JOURNEY OF DESIRE

2. GOD IS ETERNAL AND IS PRESENT EVERYWHERE . . . and because we're created in His image, we: (Reminder: you are describing positive ways we reflect our Creator, within limits.)

1 CORINTHIANS 15:53-55. For our dying bodies must be transformed into bodies that will never die; our mortal bodies must be transformed into immortal bodies. Then, when our dying bodies have been transformed into bodies that will never die, this Scripture will be fulfilled: "Death is swallowed up in victory. O death, where is your victory? O death, where is your sting?" (NLT)

2 TIMOTHY 1:9-10. This grace was given us in Christ Jesus before the beginning of time, but it has now been revealed through the appearing of our Savior, Christ Jesus, who has destroyed death and has brought life and immortality to light through the gospel.

ECCLESIASTES 3:11. God has made everything beautiful for its own time. He has planted eternity in the human heart, but even so, people cannot see the whole scope of God's work from beginning to end. (NLT)

"He hath set eternity in their heart," said the Preacher, and I think he here sets forth both the glory and the misery of men. To be made for eternity and forced to dwell in time is for mankind a tragedy of huge proportions. All within us cries for life and permanence, and everything around us reminds us of mortality and change. . . . One mark [of the divine image of God in man] may be man's insatiable craving for immortality. . . . The ancient image of God whispers within every man of everlasting hope; somewhere he will continue to exist.
— A. W. TOZER, *THE KNOWLEDGE OF THE HOLY*

3. GOD IS TRIUNE (three Persons in One) . . . and because we're created in His image, we:

GENESIS 2:18. Then the Lord God said, "It is not good for the man to be alone." (NLT)

JOHN 17:21-23. I pray that they will all be one, just as you and I are one — as you are in me, Father, and I am in you. And may they be in us so that the world will believe you sent me. I have given them the glory you gave me, so they may be one as we are one. I am in them and you are in me. (NLT)

4. GOD IS THE INDEPENDENT CREATOR . . . and because we're created in His image, we:

Our creative nature is essential to who we are as human beings — as image bearers — and it brings us great joy to live it out with freedom and skill.

— JOHN ELDREDGE, *THE JOURNEY OF DESIRE*

HABAKKUK 2:18. Of what value is an idol, since a man has carved it? Or an image that teaches lies? For he who makes it trusts in his own creation; he makes idols that cannot speak.

EPHESIANS 2:10. For we are God's workmanship, created in Christ Jesus to do good works, which God prepared in advance for us to do.

In forming our world, God spoke — and it was so. . . . He composed the symphony others merely echo and painted the portrait others reflect. He engineered the first architectural structures, called mountains and trees; programmed the first computer, called the brain; and invented the first miracle drug, called the immune system. They all started in His imagination, an imagination that has enabled our own. . . . We compose, paint, invent, write, and plan only because He did it first.

— KURT BRUNER AND JIM WARE, *FINDING GOD IN THE LAND OF NARNIA*

5. GOD IS MORALLY GOOD . . . and because we're created in His image, we:

ROMANS 2:14-15. When outsiders who have never heard of God's law follow it more or less by instinct, they confirm its truth by their obedience. They show that God's law is not something alien, imposed on us from without, but woven into the very fabric of our creation. There is something deep within them that echoes God's yes and no, right and wrong. (MSG)

1 PETER 1:16. For it is written: "Be holy, because I am holy."

6. GOD IS TRUE AND JUST . . . and because we're created in His image, we:

ISAIAH 59:11. We all growl like bears; we moan mournfully like doves. We look for justice, but find none; for deliverance, but it is far away.

ZECHARIAH 8:16. But this is what you must do: Tell the truth to each other. Render verdicts in your courts that are just and that lead to peace. (NLT)

7. GOD IS LOVE . . . and because we're created in His image, we:

1 JOHN 4:8,19. Whoever does not love does not know God, because God is love. . . . We love because he first loved us.

JOHN 15:12. My command is this: Love each other as I have loved you.

COLOSSIANS 3:14. And over all these virtues put on love, which binds them all together in perfect unity.

8. GOD IS JEALOUS . . . and because we're created in His image, we:

SONG OF SONGS 8:6-7. *Place me like a seal over your heart, like a seal on your arm. For love is as strong as death, its jealousy as enduring as the grave. Love flashes like fire, the brightest kind of flame. Many waters cannot quench love, nor can rivers drown it. If a man tried to buy love with all his wealth, his offer would be utterly scorned.* (NLT)

2 CORINTHIANS 11:2. I [Paul] am jealous for you with a godly jealousy. I promised you to one husband, to Christ, so that I might present you as a pure virgin to him.

HOSEA 3:1. The LORD said to me [Hosea], "Go, show your love to your wife again, though she is loved by another and is an adulteress. Love her as the LORD loves the Israelites, though they turn to other gods and love the sacred raisin cakes."

Hosea likens God's anger toward Israel to the anger of a husband who has just discovered that his wife has been selling herself to other men. Israel, God's bride, is a whore, and God reacts with intense jealousy.
— DR. DAN B. ALLENDER & DR. TREMPER LONGMAN III, *THE CRY OF THE SOUL*

9. GOD IS GLORIOUS AND BEAUTIFUL . . . and because we're created in His image, we:

EZEKIEL 16:14. [Speaking of the nation of Israel] And your fame spread among the nations on account of your beauty, because the splendor I had given you made your beauty perfect, declares the Sovereign LORD.

PSALM 8:4-5. What is man that you are mindful of him, the son of man that you care for him? You made him a little lower than the heavenly beings and crowned him with glory and honor.

ZECHARIAH 9:16-17. The LORD their God will save them on that day as the flock of his people. They will sparkle in his land like jewels in a crown. How attractive and beautiful they will be!

How do we begin to describe this God whose image we bear? Artistic is the only word that comes close. Power, awesome, majestic — yet intricate, delicate, whimsical. Creative, without a doubt although God rested on the seventh day, he hasn't been lying around ever since. . . . For many people this is a new thought — that God is still quite active . . . the creative overture recorded in Genesis was only the first movement of a great symphony that has been swelling ever since.

— JOHN ELDREDGE, *THE JOURNEY OF DESIRE*

From everything you have studied in this section, how do you think God and people are essentially alike?

How do you think God and people are essentially different?

PRAYER PAUSE

Pray over one of these attributes of God. Here's a suggested way to begin praying:

I praise You, Lord God, that You are _____

_____

Because _____

Thank You that—reflecting this attribute—You created me to be

_____

Please help me reflect Your image in how I live my life.

Sit in silence in His presence for a while.

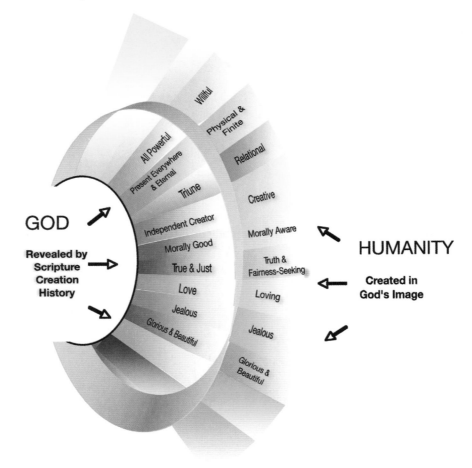

PAUSE 2_EXPLORING YOUR REALITY

Let's pause in our exploration of who God created you to be. For a few minutes, let's explore several factors other than God that can define and influence who we think we are.

OTHER PEOPLE

In a few words, how would these people describe you? (select three or four)

___ Your mother . . .

___ Your father . . .

___ Your brother/sister . . .

___ Your friends . . .

___ Your enemies . . .

___ Your boyfriend/girlfriend (if applicable) . . .

From the above, whose opinions have influenced you most? Circle them.

Who do you think has the most accurate perspective on who you are?

Who do you think has the most right to "define" who you are? Why?

How does the idea that everyone is created in the image of God affect your relationships with people who are difficult to get along with? (Think of one of those people as you respond.)

DISLIKES

Sometimes people dislike themselves. They may resent the way God made them. They may want to be something they aren't, or to change something about themselves. Are there specific things about yourself you would change if you could? Why?

Things I don't like or would change about myself:

-

-

-

WEAKNESSES AND STRUGGLES

Sometimes people allow their weaknesses to define them: "I'm a klutz . . . a nerd . . . a loser." Still others believe that their bad habits, struggles, addictions, or failures define them: "I'm an alcoholic . . . I'm hooked on food/porn/TV/spending . . . I ruined my marriage," and so forth.

My weaknesses, struggles, failures:

-

-

-

Michael Card, the songwriter, told me the biggest thing he learned from counseling was that his gift was not his identity. That he can sing and strum his guitar and create music is not his identity. "If it is, I am an idolater," he said. For many pastors, their gift is their identity; their strength is their weakness, their idol.
— LARRY CRABB, *LEADERSHIP JOURNAL*, SUMMER 2004

STRENGTHS AND ABILITIES

At the other extreme, some of us think that our strengths and abilities and roles define us: "I'm the quarterback . . . I'm a writer . . . I'm a parent." Chew on the quote about Michael Card. Then name three to four strengths, abilities, or roles of yours that you sometimes use to identify yourself.

My strengths, abilities, roles:

-
-
-

Which of these factors have you most allowed to define you? Explain.

___ Other people   ___ Weaknesses and struggles
___ Dislikes   ___ Strengths and abilities

Consider these verses about letting God — not ourselves or anyone else — define us.

> *ISAIAH 45:9-10. Woe to him who quarrels with his Maker, to him who is but a potsherd [a worthless piece of broken pottery] among the potsherds on the ground. Does the clay say to the potter, "What are you making?" Does your work say, "He has no hands"? Woe to him who says to his father, "What have you begotten?" or to his mother, "What have you brought to birth?"*

When you "quarrel with your Maker," what do you typically complain to Him about?

Consider how Paul dealt with his own weaknesses and shameful past.

> *1 CORINTHIANS 15:9-10. For I am the least of all the apostles. In fact, I'm not even worthy to be called an apostle after the way I persecuted God's church. But whatever I am now, it is all because God poured out his special favor on me — and not without results.* (NLT)

PHILIPPIANS 1:6. Being confident of this, that he who began a good work in you will carry it on to completion until the day of Christ Jesus.

What do these passages say about dealing with our weaknesses?

How do you imagine the experience of being on the potter's wheel in His hands?

ISAIAH 64:8. Yet, O LORD, you are our Father. We are the clay, you are the potter; we are all the work of your hand.

PRAYER PAUSE

This may be a great time to pause and pray. Silently go before the Father and reveal your heart to Him. Ask Him to meet with you. Name any of these influences (your dislikes, struggles, failures, etc.) that have come to define you more than they should. If you can, thank God for what they've taught you. Then tell Him that you know they don't define who you are. Talk with God about allowing Him — and only Him — to define you! Be careful not to pass by this conversation with Him.

PAUSE 3_COMING ALIVE TO GOD AND OTHERS

So we are back to the "WHO AM I?" question. Or maybe the real question should be "WHO WAS I CREATED TO BE?" Looking at the DNA similarities, some would answer that we humans are just an evolutionary inch above chimpanzees. Looking to some religions, others would say that we are all gods-in-the-making.

What really matters is what God says, because you truly are whoever and whatever He says you are. From these passages, where has God placed us (humankind collectively) in the line of created things?

> *PSALM 8:3-8.*
> *When I consider your heavens,*
> *   the work of your fingers,*
> *the moon and the stars,*
> *   which you have set in place,*
> *what is man that you are mindful of him,*
> *   the son of man that you care for him?*
> *You made him a little lower*
> *   than the heavenly beings*
> *and crowned him with glory and honor.*
> *You made him ruler over the works of your hands;*
> *   You put everything under his feet:*
> *all flocks and herds,*
> *   and the beasts of the field,*
> *the birds of the air,*
> *   and the fish of the sea,*
> *   all that swim the paths of the seas.*

> *GENESIS 1:28. God blessed them: "Prosper! Reproduce! Fill Earth! Take charge! Be responsible for fish in the sea and birds in the air, for every living thing that moves on the face of Earth."* (MSG)

Here is a truth that reaches into the deepest part of what it means to be a person. . . . That we are made to "have dominion" within an appropriate domain of reality. This is the core of the likeness or image of God in us and is the basis of the destiny for which we were formed. We are, all of us, never-ceasing spiritual beings with a unique eternal calling to count for good in God's great universe. . . . In creating human beings, God made them to rule, to reign, to have dominion in a limited sphere. Only so can they be persons.
— DALLAS WILLARD, *THE DIVINE CONSPIRACY*

In what ways do you think being created in God's image prepares us to take responsibility for ourselves, others, and nature?

Think about it: You and I have been placed at the top of God's hierarchy in creation as an expression of Him to the world. How does that make you feel?

> *EPHESIANS 2:10. He creates each of us by Christ Jesus to join him in the work he does, the good work he has gotten ready for us to do, work we had better be doing.* (MSG)

PRAYER PAUSE

In silence consider several different ways you would complete this sentence. Then pray together in your group over this.

Because God created me in His image . . . I have value! I'm not trash!

PAUSE 4_ JOURNEYING FORWARD

EPHESIANS 4:1. I . . . beg you to lead a life worthy of your calling, for you have been called by God. (NLT)

How have you experienced God this week?

Select one verse or passage that was meaningful to you this week and write it here.

We live in a world of images that deeply influence how we look at life. Choose a picture from this chapter that is meaningful or disturbing to you, and briefly explain why.

Next respond to one or more of these questions in the journal on the next page. From this study is there some . . .

PROMISE from God for me to embrace?

ACTION to take?

THOUGHT about God or life to consider?

THANKFULNESS to offer?

EMOTION to express in an honest and godly way?

RELATIONSHIP to build up or reconcile?

NEED to meet?

SINFUL action or motive to confess and forsake?

JOURNAL

CREATED IN HIS IMAGE — GENESIS 1:27

So God created man in his own image, in the image of God he created him; male and female he created them.

DIGGING DEEPER

IDENTITY PRAYERS

In each prayer mentioned below, Paul asked for three things on behalf of others. He prayed that they would: (1) see God as He truly is, (2) realize that they were created in God's image, and (3) learn to live out of who God said they were.

> COLOSSIANS 1:9-14
> EPHESIANS 1:15-23
> EPHESIANS 3:14-19

Some suggestions:

1. First put down your pen and just pray through one of these prayers for yourself.
2. Then pray through it again — but this time, pray it for someone you know.
3. Then pick up that pen and write your thoughts and heart response.
4. During the coming week, pray through the other two passages the same way.

YOUR PRAYER JOURNAL

CHAPTER 3
ADAM AND EVE'S FALL: WHAT WENT WRONG WITH THEM?

ADAM'S DIARY ONE WEEK AFTER THE FALL

Oh, my God, what have we done? It all happened so fast. One minute Father was gazing straight through our eyes into our very hearts and minds. And I like to think that He saw His own glorious reflection peeking right back at Him. Back then we thought paradise would last forever.

But now, all of our innocence is history. If only that crafty serpent hadn't entered the scene with its deceptive questions. If only we hadn't wanted to be God. If only we could go back and do it right. But now our perfect relationship with Father is over. Look where it's gotten us: ashamed, wearing clothes, full of guilt and self-condemnation, blaming and fearing each other, running for cover. Oh, my God, what have we done?

And what's going to happen to us? There is no way on earth that Eve and I can reverse the damage we've done. The only hope is for the Father to have a solution, because if we're ever to enjoy Him again, He'll have to be the One to reintroduce us to trust.

Sin is the mark that Adam and Eve passed on to their descendants, including us. Sin isn't just breaking God's rules. It is breaking God's heart.

And sin has consequences. Broken trust, shame, guilt, and condemnation — this is the human price we've all paid for sin. And the only hope to remedy all this rests on the mercy of God.

PAUSE 1_EXPLORING WHAT GOD SAYS

From the tragic story of the Fall onward, the Bible unfolds God's secret plan to teach us how to be restored and trust Him again. In chapters 1 and 2, we looked at God's goodness — and the beautiful ways in which we were created to bear His image. The problem is, instead of clearly reflecting who God is, we can only offer back a distorted and darkened carica- ture — much like the images we'd find staring back in a house of mirrors at a carnival. This distortion and whatever drives us to choose this warped image are called sin.

Explain what "sin" means from your point of view.

Sin is believing the lie that you are self-created, self-dependent, and self-sustained.

— ST. AUGUSTINE

Do you ever wonder how we got into such a mess — and where sin came from in the first place? Genesis 3–5 tells the whole story about where sin came from.

Read Genesis 3:1 through 4:8 from your Bible. As you read, search for clues on:

- What factors contributed to the world's first sin on the part of Adam and Eve.
- The impact of their sin on human nature. Write your observations below.

FACTORS CONTRIBUTING TO ADAM AND EVE'S SIN	IMPACT OF ADAM AND EVE'S SIN ON HUMAN NATURE
v. 1, 4 — Eve was naïve and not used to being deceived.	v. 4 — all of us will die.

Check out the description of the human race only two chapters later:

GENESIS 5:3; 6:5-6. When Adam was 130 years old, he became the father of a son who was just like him — in his very image. He named his son Seth. The LORD observed the extent of human wickedness on the earth, and he saw that everything they thought or imagined was consistently and totally evil. So the LORD was sorry he had ever made them and put them on the earth. It broke his heart. (NLT)

How would you describe the change in human nature from Genesis 1 to Genesis 6?

Read the following passages. Summarize your observations in the chart below.

PROVERBS 6:16-19   MARK 7:20-23   2 TIMOTHY 3:1-5

WHAT SIN **IS**	SIN'S **CONSEQUENCES**

Adam and Eve were warned about the fruit of the tree in the middle of the garden. It was their only restriction, a symbol of their freedom to accept or reject God's offer of intimacy. The tree was placed in the garden not to tempt but to testify. It stood as a daily reminder to Adam and Eve that they could enjoy God's loving protection or chart their own course. The choice was made clear. The consequences were explained. But the deception was sweet and the enticement great.

*At that fateful moment, **knowledge beyond purity** entered our existence. We quickly discovered that life apart from God is a cold, dark, barren place. And there is no turning back. The dark juice of the apple stains our face as its misery invades our lives. We got what we wanted. But we do not like it.*

— KURT BRUNER AND JIM WARE, *FINDING GOD IN THE LAND OF NARNIA*

Reflect for a moment on "knowledge beyond purity" entering your existence. If anything strikes you, write it down.

When you look at sin in this light, you can see that it's not simply about breaking a "do's and don'ts" list. Sin is about hurting God's heart. When I sin, I wound God, just like both of the sons in the parable of the prodigal son break their father's heart.

— RICHARD WAGNER, *BELIEVERITY FOR DUMMIES*

Ponder how God feels about sin and about His perfect creation being infected by imperfection. Journal your thoughts. Or write a poem or a letter to God.

PAUSE 2_EXPLORING YOUR REALITY

Before we move on, let's be sure we are on the same page by matching these terms with their definitions.

___ Guilt   ___ To Judge   ___ Forgiving
___ Sin   ___ Shame   ___ Judgmental
___ Mercy   ___ Repentance

A. To form an opinion
B. The compassionate desire to be kind and lenient toward those under one's power
C. Inclined to make judgments, especially condemning moral or personal judgments about other people
D. The act of pardoning someone's offense, releasing them from penalty, and giving up any anger or resentment
E. A painful sense of unworthiness, disgrace, or self-condemnation
F. Breaking a law or reproaching yourself for doing wrong
G. Violating God's moral standards; missing God's mark
H. Acknowledging past sins with such regret or sorrow that one turns away from sin toward God

(Answers on next page)

Do you agree with the following quotes about sin? Can you connect it to a personal experience? If so, what did you learn?

You never find in sin that which you enter the sin to find.
— Dr. James Borror

Sin always has two price tags. There's the up-front advertised price of sin, which you pay because it's worth the immediate pleasure. But then there's the price of sin's long-term consequences. That price is always higher.

— Author Unknown

CONSEQUENCE 1: *LOSS OF TRUST*

One of the "unadvertised" prices of sin is the loss of trust. What were some of Adam and Eve's issues with trust?

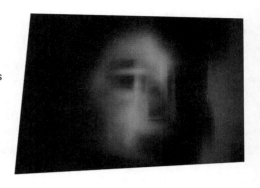

How does our sin (and others' sins against us) affect our ability to trust?

Think of a time when someone violated your trust. How did that affect your ability to trust others? To trust God?

Have you ever violated someone else's trust? If so, how did that affect that person's ability to trust you?

ANSWERS for previous page:
F-Guilt, G-Sin, B-Mercy, A-To Judge, E-Shame, H-Repentance, D-Forgiving, and C-Judgmental

PAUSE 3_COMING ALIVE TO GOD AND OTHERS

Sin has consequences — right away, as well as later on, and whether we get caught or not. Let's explore several more consequences that sin throws in our faces. We've already touched on the loss of trust. There are many others, but we'll look at three more.

CONSEQUENCE 2: GUILT

GUILT=that inner echo saying, I have done wrong. *A sense of violating a standard.*

One of sin's first consequences is often feelings of guilt. Read and mark words that describe how David experienced the pain of his guilt.

> PSALM 38:1-4.
> O LORD, don't rebuke me in your anger
>   or discipline me in your rage!
> Your arrows have struck deep,
>   and your blows are crushing me.
> Because of your anger, my whole body is sick;
>   my health is broken because of my sins.
> My guilt overwhelms me —
>   it is a burden too heavy to bear. (NLT)

David speaks of a heaviness and dirtiness that weighed on him. Can you relate at all, or remember other ways guilt has affected you?

Do you tend to feel guiltier for things you've done or for things you've failed to do?

How do you deal with feelings of guilt?

CONƧEQUENCE 3: ƧHAME

SHAME=that inner echo saying, I am flawed. *A sense of a deep unworthiness.*

This consequence of sin — shame — attacks who we are in light of what we've done. It convinces us that there is something deeply wrong with us. "No one will ever want me in my condition!"

In your experience, what things make you feel flawed or unworthy? What specifically triggers this powerful emotion?

This verse may help us see shame and guilt together. Try paraphrasing this verse in your own words:

ROMANS 3:23. For all have sinned [guilt] and fall short of the glory of God [shame].

> *If you <u>bury</u> your guilt and shame alive . . .*
> - *They become a <u>bomb</u> waiting to explode!*
> - *They spawn a <u>belief</u> that you're hopelessly flawed.*

The reality of shame is driven by the fear of being exposed for who I really am in all my imperfection, instead of people and God seeing the person I want them to think I am. Our instinct is to hide at all costs rather than being seen.

Read GENESIS 2:25 through 3:10. Before they sinned, Adam and Eve were "naked and unashamed." But after they sinned, they hid from God and tried to cover themselves. Why do you think Adam and Eve hid from God?

Adam and Eve covered themselves with leaves. God covered them with garments of skins. We cover ourselves with clothes every day. Why?

Are you ever conscious of hiding from yourself?

Imagine what would have happened to Adam and Eve if they were not given the capacity to feel guilt and shame. Would they — or the rest of the human race — be better off without these emotions?

Consider a different angle on shame.

PSALM 83:16-18.
Utterly disgrace them [God's wicked enemies]
  until they submit to your name, O LORD.
Let them be ashamed and terrified forever.
  Let them die in disgrace.
Then they will learn that you alone are called the LORD,
  that you alone are the Most High,
  supreme over all the earth. (NLT)

Here we see God's willingness to use a consequence of sin to ultimately bring our hearts full circle back to Him. From this passage, how can shame contribute to your spiritual growth?

CONƧEQUENCE 4: condemnation

OTHERS	SATAN
GOD	SELF

Condemnation seems to come at us from all sides. God has a right to condemn us because we deserve it. Fortunately, His mercy moved Him to provide Christ to free us from His condemnation. But other voices whisper that we don't deserve His mercy. Just step out of line an inch, and sometimes we will condemn ourselves; sometimes others condemn us. And you can be sure that Satan will always live up to his name: the Accuser!

CONDEMNATION FROM GOD

Since sin is a capital crime in the eyes of our holy God, it always deserves the capital punishment: death. God is morally perfect and He has rights as the Sovereign Creator. So He always judges people from His holy nature.

In these passages, circle and summarize whatever you notice about sin's consequences.

EZEKIEL 7:27. I will deal with them according to their conduct, and by their own standards I will judge them. Then they will know that I am the LORD.

ROMANS 5:12. When Adam sinned, sin entered the world. Adam's sin brought death, so death spread to everyone, for everyone sinned. (NLT)

HEBREWS 9:27. And just as each person is destined to die once and after that comes judgment. (NLT)

Who would you rather have judge you for your sins — people or God? Why?

How do you feel about God judging people by His standards? By their own standards?

CONDEMNATION FROM OTHERS

God isn't the only one doing some judging in this world. Every one of us has heard other voices of condemnation whispering accusations in our ear.

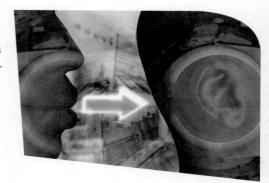

Think of a specific time when someone judged or condemned you. How did you feel?

What may have been true — and false — about this judgment?

Is this condemnation still affecting you? Explain.

Humanity was made in God's image, so we are able to make judgments. Judging can be our legitimate way to bring fairness (as in court cases) or to make sound decisions (as in judging a candidate's suitability for office).

Unfortunately our sinful nature has so badly marred God's image in us that we tend to view what's fair from our imperfect, temporary, often self-serving point of view. Before we know it, we've crossed the line from healthy discernment into illegitimate judging (scorning the divorced, despising the obese, shaming the unemployed or homeless, condemning the adulterer, etc.). We find ourselves trying to take over God's role and doing the judging for Him. And then we've become judgmental.

To keep us from becoming judgmental of others, what guidelines do you see about judging from this verse?

GUIDELINES: *ROMANS 2:1. You, therefore, have no excuse, you who*
                                         pass judgment on someone else, for at whatever point
                                         you judge the other, you are condemning yourself,
                                         because you who pass judgment do the same things.

List those areas where you tend to be most judgmental of others.

CONDEMNATION FROM SELF AND SATAN

God designed our conscience to act as an inner voice, something to speak up before we mess up. But once we have been forgiven by the Divine, we need to silence the accusing voices within us and listen to the words of grace. Satan, too, nags at our thoughts to make us believe his lies.

What advice do you find in the following verses to help you deal with condemnation from yourself or from Satan?

REVELATION 12:10-11. Then I heard a loud voice in heaven say: "Now have come the salvation and the power and the kingdom of our God, and the authority of his Christ. For the accuser of our brothers [Satan], who accuses them before our God day and night, has been hurled down. They overcame him by the blood of the Lamb and by the word of their testimony; they did not love their lives so much as to shrink from death."

1 JOHN 3:18-19. My dear children, let's not just talk about love; let's practice real love. This is the only way we'll know we're living truly, living in God's reality. It's also the way to shut down debilitating self-criticism, even when there is something to it. For God is greater than our worried hearts and knows more about us than we do ourselves. (MSG)

WHEN JESUS TOUCHES OUR SHAME

If you would like to read a story where these consequences of sin come together and Jesus responds to guilt, shame, and condemnation, read the story of the Samaritan woman in John 4:5-38. What do you think was her experience in terms of:

Sense of Trust:

Sense of Loss:

Sense of Guilt:

Sense of Shame:

Sense of Condemnation by Others:

Sense of Self-Condemnation:

How did Jesus deal with the Samaritan woman's guilt, shame, and condemnation?

How does it make you feel to realize that Jesus has every reason to condemn, reject, and abandon you — but doesn't?

PRAYER PAUSE

Recall those things that make you feel ashamed, guilty, or condemned. In a time of prayer, ask God how He might want you to respond to your feelings in ways that lead you to Him. Thank God for these emotions. Ask Him for wisdom to discern true guilt and shame while drawing closer to Him.

Read ROMANS 8:1. How has Jesus touched your heart regarding your sense of trust, guilt, shame, and condemnation?

PAUSE 4_JOURNEYING FORWARD

EPHESIANS 4:1. I . . . beg you to lead a life worthy of your calling, for you have been called by God. (NLT)

How have you experienced God this week?

Select one verse or passage that was meaningful to you this week and write it here.

We live in a world of images that deeply influence how we look at life. Choose a picture from this chapter that is meaningful or disturbing to you, and briefly explain why.

Next respond to one or more of these questions in the journal on the next page. From this study is there some . . .

PROMISE from God for me to embrace?

ACTION to take?

THOUGHT about God or life to consider?

THANKFULNESS to offer?

EMOTION to express in an honest and godly way?

RELATIONSHIP to build up or reconcile?

NEED to meet?

SINFUL action or motive to confess and forsake?

JOURNAL

CHAPTER 4
ADAM AND EVE'S MARK: WHAT'S WRONG WITH ME?

"What's wrong with me?" Keiko has asked herself that question maybe a thousand times. When she looks around, she also wonders, "What's wrong with that person?"

It's obvious that something is seriously wrong with human nature. But identifying what's wrong is more difficult. Frankly, Keiko's main concern is with herself. She's so confused about how she can be so compassionate one moment and then makes such critical remarks the next moment. More and more lately she realizes that she sounds like her mom! Where does all this inner garbage come from? Is all this hereditary?

Freedom to live out God's design involves an honest look at how broken we truly are. Only in dealing honestly with the shame, sin, and wounding that shroud God's image in us can we begin to emerge out of our brokenness.
— PARAPHRASED FROM ANDREW COMISKEY, *STRENGTH IN WEAKNESS*

What do you think it means to be "broken"?

How broken do you feel most of the time? Explain.

PAUSE 1_EXPLORING WHAT GOD SAYS

The apostle Paul gives us a tell-it-like-it-is history of sin in his letter to the Romans in chapter 1. He says there is a direct relationship between what people think about God and what they give themselves permission to do. As the first deteriorates, so does the second. He could be describing the downward spiral of a culture, as well as a person.

As you meditate on this passage, mark it up with underlining, circles, or colored pens as you go. On the following chart:

1. Mark what you notice about the decline of thoughts and attitudes toward God.
2. Use the left column to summarize in your own words. Here are some starting observations.

THOUGHTS AND ATTITUDES TOWARD GOD	ROMANS 1:18–2:1
Knowledge of God was built into creation Suppressed the truth about God Didn't honor or thank God	¹⁸ The wrath of God is being revealed from heaven against all the godlessness and wickedness of men who <u>suppress the truth</u> by their wickedness, since <u>what may be known about God is plain</u> to them, because God has made it plain to them. For since the creation of the world God's invisible qualities — his eternal power and divine nature — have been clearly seen, <u>being understood from what has been made</u>, so that men are without excuse. ²¹ For although they knew God, they <u>neither glorified him as God</u> nor <u>gave thanks to him</u>, but their thinking became futile and their foolish hearts were darkened. Although they claimed to be wise, they became fools and exchanged the glory of the immortal God for images made to look like mortal man and birds and animals and reptiles. ²⁴ Therefore God gave them over in the sinful desires of their hearts to sexual impurity for the degrading of their bodies with one another. They exchanged the truth of God for a lie, and worshiped and served created things rather than the Creator — who is forever praised. Amen. ²⁶ Because of this, God gave them over to shameful lusts. Even their women exchanged natural relations for unnatural ones. In the same way the men also abandoned natural relations with women and

THOUGHTS AND ATTITUDES TOWARD GOD (con't)	ROMANS 1:18–2:1 (con't)
	were inflamed with lust for one another. Men committed indecent acts with other men, and received in themselves the due penalty for their perversion. 28 Furthermore, since they did not think it worthwhile to retain the knowledge of God, he gave them over to a depraved mind, to do what ought not to be done. They have become filled with every kind of wickedness, evil, greed and depravity. They are full of envy, murder, strife, deceit and malice. They are gossips, slanderers, God-haters, insolent, arrogant and boastful; they invent ways of doing evil; they disobey their parents; they are senseless, faithless, heartless, ruthless. Although they know God's righteous decree that those who do such things deserve death, they not only continue to do these very things but also approve of those who practice them. 2:1 You, therefore, have no excuse, you who pass judgment on someone else, for at whatever point you judge the other, you are condemning yourself, because you who pass judgment do the same things.

Now read this passage again from *The Message*. This time:

1. Mark anything you notice about the degeneration of human behavior and actions.
2. Summarize what you discover in the right column. We'll get you started on the first few verses.

ROMANS 1:18–2:1 (THE SAME PASSAGE AGAIN FROM *THE MESSAGE* TRANSLATION)	BEHAVIOR/ACTIONS
18 But God's angry displeasure erupts as acts of human mistrust and wrongdoing and lying accumulate, as people try to put a shroud over truth. But the basic reality of God is plain enough. Open your eyes and there it is! By taking a long and thoughtful look at what God has created, people have always been able to see what their eyes as such can't see: eternal power, for instance, and the mystery of his divine being. So nobody has a good excuse. 21 What happened was this: People knew God perfectly well, but when they didn't treat him like God, refusing to worship him, they	Piled up all kinds of wrong acts like lying and mistrust

trivialized themselves into silliness and confusion so that there was neither sense nor direction left in their lives. They pretended to know it all, but were illiterate regarding life. They traded the glory of God who holds the whole world in his hands for cheap figurines you can buy at any roadside stand.

²⁴ So God said, in effect, "If that's what you want, that's what you get." It wasn't long before they were living in a pigpen, smeared with filth, filthy inside and out. And all this because they traded the true God for a fake god, and worshiped the god they made instead of the God who made them—the God we bless, the God who blesses *us*. Oh, yes!

²⁶ Worse followed. Refusing to know God, they soon didn't know how to be human either—women didn't know how to be women, men didn't know how to be men. Sexually confused, they abused and defiled one another, women with women, men with men—all lust, no love. And then they paid for it, oh, how they paid for it—emptied of God and love, godless and loveless wretches.

²⁸ Since they didn't bother to acknowledge God, God quit bothering them and let them run loose. And then all hell broke loose: rampant evil, grabbing and grasping, vicious backstabbing. They made life hell on earth with their envy, wanton killing, bickering, and cheating. Look at them: mean-spirited, venomous, fork-tongued God-bashers. Bullies, swaggerers, insufferable windbags! They keep inventing new ways of wrecking lives. They ditch their parents when they get in the way. Stupid, slimy, cruel, cold-blooded. And it's not as if they don't know better. They know perfectly well they're spitting in God's face. And they don't care—worse, they hand out prizes to those who do the worst things best!

²:¹ Those people are on a dark spiral downward. But if you think that leaves you on the high ground where you can point your finger at others, think again. Every time you criticize someone, you condemn yourself.

Three times, the NIV passage says that God "gave them over" to their sinful desires. What do you think that means?

One principle from this passage is: What we think about God influences what we give ourselves permission to do. Can you illustrate this from your life?

SUMMARY

Let's try to summarize visually what we've discovered from Scripture. On the right we have listed just a few of God's attributes revealed to us through the "prisms" of Scripture and creation. God created humankind to reflect those attributes. But from the Fall of Adam and Eve onward, sin has marred God's image in us, like looking into a cracked and broken mirror. We look at life through the "prism" of our inherited sinful nature, so it's no wonder we feel disillusioned, disoriented, and discontent so much of the time.

Review your study of Romans 1:18 through 2:1. Add as many descriptive words as you can to the prism illustration below that express how fallen humanity has been marred by sin.

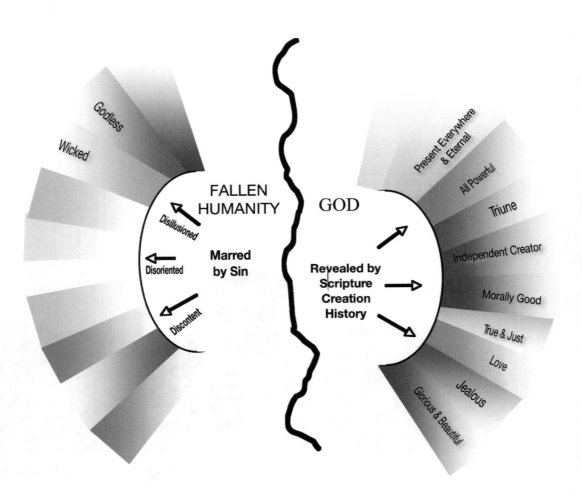

PAUSE 2_EXPLORING YOUR REALITY

Let's connect some really big dots about our design and identity as humans. Here's our working list of some of God's attributes, as well as how He designed us to reflect His image. Describe in a sentence or two <u>how you think our sin nature has marred our original intended design</u>. Again, you can do them all, or select the ones you are most interested in. We'll get you started.

1. God is ALL POWERFUL .... We are BEHAVIORAL ....
   But Sin . . . Sin makes us focus our behaviors and purposes toward our own selfish interests first; sin makes us think, "Hey, if I can get away with it, why not?"

2. God is PRESENT EVERYWHERE & ETERNAL .... We are PHYSICAL & FINITE ....
   But Sin . . .

3. God is TRIUNE (three Persons in One) .... We are RELATIONAL ....
   But Sin . . .

4. God is INDEPENDENT CREATOR .... We are CREATIVE ....
   But Sin . . .

5. God is MORALLY GOOD .... We are MORALLY AWARE ....
   But Sin . . .

6. God is TRUE & JUST .... We SEEK TRUTH & FAIRNESS ....
   But Sin . . .

7. God is LOVE .... We are LOVING ....
   But Sin . . .

8. God is JEALOUS for us .... We are JEALOUS for those we love ....
   But Sin . . .

9. God is GLORIOUS & BEAUTIFUL .... We are GLORIOUS & BEAUTIFUL ....
   But Sin . . .

What do you realize about how sin has messed with your identity?

PAUSE 3_COMING ALIVE TO GOD AND OTHERS

Bad shame invites the soul to turn on itself rather than to welcome mercy. . . . Good shame alerts us to our separation from God and others, potentially causing us to cry out to God for mercy. And when we do so, God replaces our fig leaves with robes of righteousness — garments that lend form and order to our relationships.
— ANDREW COMISKEY, STRENGTH IN WEAKNESS

So far, we've looked at the bad news. NOW HERE'S THE GOOD NEWS: the hope for our rescue is found in God's mercy. Read these two stories to find out how four different people experienced (or didn't experience) God's mercy covering their guilt and shame. In each story ask yourself who did (and didn't) struggle with shame? Who did (and didn't) experience mercy?

LUKE 7:36-48. [Jesus] went to the Pharisee's house and sat down at the dinner table. Just then a woman of the village, the town harlot, having learned that Jesus was a guest in the home of the Pharisee, came with a bottle of very expensive perfume and stood at his feet, weeping, raining tears on his feet. . . .

⁴⁰ Jesus said to [the Pharisee], "Simon, I have something to tell you."

"Oh? Tell me."

⁴¹⁻⁴² "Two men were in debt to a banker. One owed five hundred silver pieces, the other fifty. Neither of them could pay up, and so the banker canceled both debts. Which of the two would be more grateful?"

Simon answered, "I suppose the one who was forgiven the most."

⁴³⁻⁴⁷ "That's right," said Jesus. Then turning to the woman, but speaking to Simon, he said, "Do you see this woman? I came to your home; you provided no water for my feet, but she rained tears on my feet and dried them with her hair. You gave me no greeting, but from the time I arrived she hasn't quit kissing my feet. . . . Impressive, isn't it? She was forgiven many, many sins, and so she is very, very grateful. If the forgiveness is minimal, the gratitude is minimal."

⁴⁸ Then he spoke to her: "I forgive your sins." (MSG)

LUKE 18:9-14. [Jesus] told his next story to some who were complacently pleased with themselves over their moral performance and looked down their noses at the common people. "Two men went up to the Temple to pray, one a Pharisee, the other a tax man. The Pharisee posed and prayed like this: 'Oh, God, I thank you that I am not like other people — robbers, crooks, adulterers, or heaven forbid, like this tax man. I fast twice a week and tithe on all my income.'

13 "Meanwhile the tax man, slumped in the shadows, his face in his hands, not daring to look up, said, 'God, give mercy. Forgive me, a sinner.'"

14 Jesus commented, "This tax man, not the other, went home made right with God. If you walk around with your nose in the air, you're going to end up flat on your face, but if you're content to be simply yourself, you will become more than yourself." (MSG)

WHAT IS MERCY?
It is that part of God's character that holds back His hand of condemnation because He jealously loves us.

Imagine that you are either the adoring woman or the tax collector.

How do you think she or he felt about experiencing God's mercy?

What other good things do you think she or he experienced? Try writing as though she or he is speaking.

Now think about Simon and the Pharisee at the temple. What was it that prevented them from experiencing God's mercy and forgiveness? What else did they miss out on? (Again, try writing as though he is speaking.)

What obstacles might prevent you from experiencing God's mercy?

Both stories illustrate mercy leading to forgiveness. Mark whatever you observe about mercy and forgiveness. In the margin express how you feel about this.

**FEELINGS ABOUT MERCY
AND FORGIVENESS**

LAMENTATIONS 3:22-23. The LORD's lovingkindnesses indeed never cease, for His compassions never fail. They are new every morning; great is Your faithfulness. (NASB)

PSALM 145:9. The LORD is good to all, and His mercies are over all His works. (NASB)

JAMES 2:13. Because judgment without mercy will be shown to anyone who has not been merciful. Mercy triumphs over judgment!

1 PETER 2:9-10. But you are not like that, for you are a chosen people. You are royal priests, a holy nation, God's very own possession. As a result, you can show others the goodness of God, for he called you out of the darkness into his wonderful light. "Once you had no identity as a people; now you are God's people. Once you received no mercy; now you have received God's mercy." (NLT)

What would happen if there were no such thing as mercy?

What difference has mercy (from God or others) made in your life?

TAKE SOME TIME TO PRAY

PRAYER SUGGESTIONS

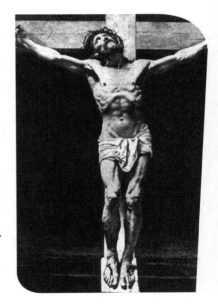

1. Be silent before Him.
2. Meditate on the quotation and painting on this page.
3. Talk to God about the consequences you've experienced because of sin — your own sin and the sin of others.
4. Talk about your capacity to receive His mercy and love.
5. Talk to God about the price He paid for your sin through Jesus on the cross.
6. Ask Him for a deeper sense of His presence in ordinary life and a deeper sense of His mercy and jealous love for you — and thank Him for this.

Take some time to pray together as a group.

It's a wonder God didn't lose his temper and do away with the whole lot of us. Instead, immense in mercy and with an incredible love, he embraced us. He took our sin-dead lives and made us alive in Christ. He did all this on his own, with no help from us! Then he picked us up and set us down in highest heaven in company with Jesus, our Messiah. (EPHESIANS 2:3-6, MSG)

PAUSE 4_JOURNEYING FORWARD

EPHESIANS 4:1. I . . . beg you to lead a life worthy of your calling, for you have been called by God. (NLT)

How have you experienced God this week?

Select one verse or passage that was meaningful to you this week and write it here.

We live in a world of images that deeply influence how we look at life. Choose a picture from this chapter that is meaningful or disturbing to you, and briefly explain why.

Next respond to one or more of these questions in the journal on the next page. From this study is there some . . .

PROMISE from God for me to embrace?

ACTION to take?

THOUGHT about God or life to consider?

THANKFULNESS to offer?

EMOTION to express in an honest and godly way?

RELATIONSHIP to build up or reconcile?

NEED to meet?

SINFUL action or motive to confess and forsake?

JOURNAL

SUGGESTED MEMORY VERSE:

MERCY FOR SIN — LAMENTATIONS 3:22-23 (NRSV)

The steadfast love of the LORD never ceases, his mercies never come to an end; they are new every morning; great is thy faithfulness.

78

CHAPTER 5

TRANSFORMING INTO JESUS' IMAGE:
WHAT'S NEW ABOUT ME?

Elena's life before Christ was a mess. Childhood sexual abuse had left tremendous scars. In many ways the abuse had defined who she imagined she was: an object deserving abuse, a beauty to be defiled, a soul ready to be tormented, a child not to be protected.

To Elena, God's amazing promise to make her completely new in Christ was overwhelming. Tenderly, Jesus began to expose and strip away the "old things" like old clothes that didn't fit her anymore:

- *consequences of abuse at the hands of others*
- *soul baggage accumulated by her own choices and actions*
- *a crushing weight of guilt, shame, anger, and fear*

He was holding out "new things." New God-given robes of righteousness through Jesus began to cover her! She sensed new meaning for all she'd suffered, refreshing peace, assurance and love, and a new sense of stable joy.

But in truth, Elena was still skeptical. The promise of becoming new in Christ seemed too good to be true, at least for someone like her. If all her feelings of worthlessness didn't go away, would that mean she really wasn't new in Christ? Then who would define her? Her abusers? Herself? Or Jesus? She wondered just how long it would take for the old things to pass away.

PAUSE 1_EXPLORING WHAT GOD SAYS

The contrast between God's way of doing things and our way is never more acute than in this area of human change and transformation. We focus on specific actions; God focuses on us. We work from the outside in; God works from the inside out. We try; God transforms.

— RICHARD FOSTER, *DEVOTIONAL CLASSICS*

We spent the last two chapters looking at the mess that the first Adam got us all into. At long last, we've arrived at Jesus' Good News! Jesus — the "second Adam" — is the way home, back to experiencing life with our Father as He intended it to be. Jesus redeems us from sin, reconciles us to God, and is now restoring the image of God that we all bear.

As you study this passage from Romans, write your observations in the columns. Consider highlighting these themes in two different colors as you meditate.

- **Left column:** Adam and the impact of his sin
- **Right column:** Christ and the impact of His obedience

ADAM'S IMPACT	ROMANS 5:12-21 (NLT)	CHRIST'S IMPACT
His sin infected all humans with sin & sentenced all of us to death	[12] When Adam sinned, sin entered the world. Adam's sin brought death, so death spread to everyone, for everyone sinned. [13] Yes, people sinned even before the law was given. But it was not counted as sin because there was not yet any law to break. [14] Still, everyone died — from the time of Adam to the time of Moses — even those who did not disobey an explicit commandment of God, as Adam did. Now Adam is a symbol, a representation of Christ, who was yet to come. [15] But there is a great difference between Adam's sin and God's gracious gift. For the sin of this one man, Adam, brought death to many. But even greater is God's wonderful grace and his gift of forgiveness to many through this other man, Jesus Christ. [16] And the result of God's gracious gift is very different from the result of that one man's sin. For Adam's sin led to condemnation, but God's	

ADAM'S IMPACT (con't)	ROMANS 5:12-21 (NLT) (con't)	CHRIST'S IMPACT (con't)
	free gift leads to our being made right with God, even though we are guilty of many sins. . . . 18 Yes, Adam's one sin brings condemnation for everyone, but Christ's one act of righteousness brings a right relationship with God and new life for everyone. Because one person disobeyed God, many became sinners. But because one other person obeyed God, many will be made righteous. 20 God's law was given so that all people could see how sinful they were. But as people sinned more and more, God's wonderful grace became more abundant. So just as sin ruled over all people and brought them to death, now God's wonderful grace rules instead, giving us right standing with God and resulting in eternal life through Jesus Christ our Lord.	

Reconciliation is a passion for God. This passion is embodied in his son, Jesus, who is called the last Adam — the Life-giver. Just as God breathed into the womb of the earth to bring life to the first Adam, Jesus was conceived by God in the womb of a young Jewish girl. Whereas the first Adam left the Garden of Genesis in separation from God, the Garden of Gethsemane was where Jesus embraced his redemptive work that made our restoration possible. Whereas spiritual death was introduced through the first Adam, the second Adam brings spiritual life.

— JONATHAN AND JENNIFER CAMPBELL, *THE WAY OF JESUS*

The following is a fantastic before-and-after description of us from Ephesians 2. Paul is writing to outsiders who became insiders through Christ.

- **Left column:** Summarize life without Christ
- **Right column:** Summarize life in Christ

BACKGROUND:

In Jesus' day, the devout Jews were the religious "insiders" and the rest of the people (called Gentiles) were considered "outsiders" to the knowledge of the true God. And, as you might expect, there was lots of friction between the two groups. Sound familiar?

LIFE WITHOUT CHRIST (OLD IDENTITY)	EPHESIANS 2:1-22	LIFE IN CHRIST (NEW IDENTITY)
• Stuck in habits of sin • Let the world tell me how to live	¹⁻⁶ It wasn't so long ago that you were <u>mired in that old stagnant life of sin</u>. You let the world, which doesn't know the first thing about living, <u>tell you how to live</u>. You filled your lungs with polluted unbelief, and then exhaled disobedience. We all did it, all of us doing what we felt like doing, when we felt like doing it, all of us in the same boat. It's a wonder God didn't lose his temper and do away with the whole lot of us. Instead, immense in mercy and with an incredible love, <u>he embraced us</u>. He took our sin-dead lives and <u>made us alive</u> in Christ. He did all this on his own, with no help from us! Then he picked us up and set us down in highest heaven in company with Jesus, our Messiah. . . . ¹¹⁻¹³ But don't take any of this for granted. It was only yesterday that you outsiders to God's ways had no idea of any of this, didn't know the first thing about the way God works, hadn't the faintest idea of Christ. You knew nothing of that rich history of God's covenants and promises in Israel, hadn't a clue about what God was doing in the world at large. Now because of Christ—dying that death, shedding that blood—you who were once out of it altogether are in on everything. ¹⁴⁻¹⁵ The Messiah has made things up between us so that we're now together on this, both non-Jewish outsiders and Jewish insiders. He tore down the wall we used to keep each other at a distance. He repealed the law code that had become so clogged with fine print and footnotes that it hindered more than it helped. Then he started over. Instead of continuing with two groups of people separated by centuries of animosity and suspicion, he created a new kind of human being, a fresh start for everybody. ¹⁶⁻¹⁸ Christ brought us together through his	• God embraces me • Brought me back to life again

LIFE WITHOUT CHRIST (OLD IDENTITY)	EPHESIANS 2:1-22 (con't)	LIFE IN CHRIST (NEW IDENTITY)
	death on the cross. The Cross got us to embrace, and that was the end of the hostility. Christ came and preached peace to you outsiders and peace to us insiders. He treated us as equals, and so made us equals. Through him we both share the same Spirit and have equal access to the Father. 19-22 That's plain enough, isn't it? You're no longer wandering exiles. This kingdom of faith is now your home country. You're no longer strangers or outsiders. You *belong* here, with as much right to the name Believer as anyone. God is building a home. He's using us all—irrespective of how we got here—in what he is building. He used the apostles and prophets for the foundation. Now he's using you, fitting you in brick by brick, stone by stone, with Christ Jesus as the cornerstone that holds all the parts together. We see it taking shape day after day—a holy temple built by God, all of us built into it, a temple in which God is quite at home. (MSG)	

This passage is filled with metaphors, as though Paul was grasping for words to describe what it's like to be recreated in Jesus' image. Can you find some of them? Paul compared:

OLD LIFE WITHOUT CHRIST TO:	NEW LIFE IN CHRIST TO:
breathing in polluted air	

How do you feel about who God says you are (your new identity in Christ)? What does it do for your sense of personal beauty and purpose?

Esse quam vider:
To be, rather than to appear.

PAUSE 2_EXPLORING YOUR REALITY

THE CROSS AS SHAME'S CURE

On the cross God in Christ endured the ultimate humiliation. For our weaknesses and shame, God allowed himself to become weak and full of shame. God was strung up naked before a mocking, jeering public. He subjected himself to the worst kind of exposure in order to make a way for us, his creation, who have been subject to the exposure of sin and shame ourselves. The Scripture tells us that Christ, "for the joy set before him endured the cross, scorning its shame. . . . Consider him who endured such opposition from sinful men, so that you will not grow weary and lose heart" (Heb. 12:2-3).

— ANDREW COMISKEY, *STRENGTH IN WEAKNESS*

2 CORINTHIANS 5:17. Therefore, if anyone is in Christ, he is a new creation; the old has gone, the new has come!

1 PETER 1:3. Praise be to the God and Father of our Lord Jesus Christ! In his great mercy he has given us new birth into a living hope through the resurrection of Jesus Christ from the dead.

What did you "look like" before and after Christ redeemed you? (And remember to be real. None of us is there yet. We're all in process.) Either write a metaphor, or illustrate in your own way your before-and-after Christ reality.

MY OLD LIFE WITHOUT CHRIST WAS . . .	MY NEW LIFE WITH CHRIST IS . . .

Remember those consequences of sin we all feel: loss of trust, guilt, shame, and condemnation? What happens to them when we are "in Christ"? Describe this either in words, or try drawing a picture with you and Jesus in it, illustrating this truth.

> *Living in awareness of our belovedness is the axis around which the Christian life revolves. Being the beloved is our identity, the core of our existence. It is not merely a lofty thought. It is the name by which God knows us, and the way he relates to us.*
> — BRENNAN MANNING, *THE RABBI'S HEARTBEAT*

When Jesus was baptized, He heard His Father speak these words to Him:

LUKE 3:22. And along with the Spirit, a voice: "You are my Son, chosen and marked by my love, pride of my life." (MSG)

LUKE 3:22. And a voice from heaven said, "You are my dearly loved Son, and you bring me great joy." (NLT)

What would it feel like for you to hear your heavenly Father affirm you this way? To what degree do you sense He is affirming you this way today?

PRAYER PAUSE

Consider this idea: "Confession is a first and necessary step back to the Garden, back to the place where we can be 'naked and feel no shame.' . . . Confession is presenting our real self to God. It's bringing before God not the person we hope to be, but the person we actually are" (from Mark Buchanan, *Your God Is Too Safe*).

Pause for a time of prayer, talking honestly with God about the person you actually are right now, and listening for whatever words of affirmation He might speak to you. If there are things you need to confess and turn from, do that now.

PAUSE 3_COMING ALIVE TO GOD AND OTHERS

You may be thinking, This is all good, but how I feel about who I am doesn't always match what I know about who I really am in Christ! That's okay. On the journey of spiritual transformation, feelings may lag behind awareness and understanding. So be patient with yourself. God is passionate about transforming all parts of you. He will help you embrace your belovedness in Christ. As you read through this list:

- Circle three feelings from the left column that you have struggled with most.
- Circle three truths from the right column that encourage you most about your identity in Christ.

FEELING MY FALLEN IDENTITY *(What I feel about myself)*	EMBRACING MY TRANSFORMING IDENTITY *(What is true about me)*
I may feel flawed.	I am becoming like Christ. (2 Corinthians 3:18; 1 John 3:2-3)
I may feel soul ugly.	I am beautifully adorned in Him. (Luke 15:11-24; Song of Solomon 7:6)
I may feel futile.	I am a productive citizen of the kingdom of God. (Ephesians 2:10; Colossians 3:23-25)
I may feel unlovable.	I am beloved by God. (Deuteronomy 33:12; John 15:12; 2 Thessalonians 2:13)
I may feel discontent.	I am grateful for God's work in me. (2 Corinthians 2:14-16; 1 Corinthians 15:57)
I may feel powerless.	I am empowered by the Holy Spirit. (Ephesians 3:16-21; 2 Peter 1:3-4)
I may feel meaningless.	I am meaningful in light of eternity. (2 Corinthians 5:10; 2 Timothy 4:8)
I may feel fragmented.	I am integrated by the God of all. (Colossians 1:15-20; Revelation 4:9-11)

I may feel undesirable. ⟶	I am desired by the One who calls me to Himself. (Song of Solomon 7:10)
I may feel abandoned. ⟶	I am an adopted child of God. (Ephesians 1:5; Ezekiel 16)
I may feel dishonored. ⟶	I am honored in His eyes. (Romans 2:9-11; Isaiah 43:4)
I may feel unworthy. ⟶	I am made worthy. (2 Thessalonians 1:5)
I may feel unappreciated. ⟶	I am appreciated and delighted in by God. (Psalm 18:19; Hebrews 13:16)
I may feel dirty. ⟶	I am cleansed by the blood of Christ. (Hebrews 9:13)
I may feel alone. ⟶	I am never alone for God is present with me and everywhere. (Hebrews 13:5; Psalm 37:28-29)
I may feel numb or dead. ⟶	I am alive now and eternally. (1 Peter 3:18; Romans 6:11; Ephesians 2:4-5)
I may feel rejected. ⟶	I am accepted as I am. (1 Corinthians 15:10; Romans 15:7)
I may feel disconnected. ⟶	I am connected to the body of Christ. (Ephesians 2:18-22; Colossians 1:18)
I may feel guilty. ⟶	I am forgiven. (1 John 1:9; Psalm 103:8-14)
I may feel spiritually oppressed. ⟶	I am delivered from Satan's hold. (1 John 2:14; Revelation 12:11)
I may feel condemned. ⟶	I am not condemned. (Romans 8:1; 1 John 3:19-22)
I may feel fearful. ⟶	I am at peace in God's presence. (John 14:27; John 16:33)
I may feel in bondage. ⟶	I am free in Christ. (Galatians 5:1,13-14)
I may feel like a failure. ⟶	I am gifted because of God's unique design of me. (Ephesians 4:11-13; 1 Corinthians 12:1-31; Romans 12:6-8; 1 Peter 4:10-11)

I may feel disillusioned. ———————→ I am real in Christ. (1 John 2:27-28; Romans 9:1-2; 1 Timothy 1:5-6)

I may feel inadequate. ———————→ I am adequate in Jesus. (2 Corinthians 3:4-5; 1 Corinthians 15:10)

I may feel ashamed. ———————→ I am unashamed in God's presence because Jesus took my shame. (Hebrews 12:2; Hebrews 11:16)

I may feel depressed. ———————→ I am given joy in Jesus. (1 Peter 1:8; John 16:24)

Why not try this creative approach in your time alone with God? Each day, chew on one truth from the above list about your transformed identity. Then meditate on the Bible passages provided, and invite the Lord to help you understand, accept, and embrace your transforming identity in Christ.

MY NEW IDENTITY IN CHRIST

PROCESSING TIME: If you haven't already done so, go back and circle three feelings from the left column that you have struggled with in the past or are struggling with now. The difficult emotions you circled probably reveal needs in your heart that the Lord would like to bring more comfort and healing to — if you will let Him. Maybe one or more of these needs is on the front line of His ongoing ministry to transform your life. Here is a simple process combining prayer and the Word that invites the Lord to help you understand, accept, and embrace your transforming identity in Christ.

- I have struggled with feeling (select one feeling you circled from the left column):

- Write to God what's on your heart about this feeling.

- Despite what you feel, write what God says is true about you (from the right column):

- Look up the related Scripture passages provided and summarize the key truth in each:

  <u>Verse Reference</u>   <u>Key Truth About Me</u>

- Share with God your response to these truths. Ask Him to help you embrace your true identity. Journal:

TIME ALONE WITH GOD

During the remaining weeks of this study, why not try this creative approach in your daily time alone with God? Each day, chew on one truth about your identity from the list (pages 87 through 89) by expressing how you feel to your Father. Then meditate on the Bible passages provided, and invite the Lord to help you understand and embrace your transforming identity in Christ. Use the following ideas to process your true identity, writing your responses in a journal.

Select one feeling I have struggled with.
Write to God what's on my heart about this feeling.
What God says is true about me (from the Bible).
Look up related Bible verses, and summarize the key truths in each.
Share with God my response to these truths.
Ask Him to help me embrace my true identity.

COMMUNITY AFFIRMATION

Take time as a group to affirm each other out loud from the list of "I am . . ." truths on pages 87 through 89. Go around your group (several times), each affirming the next person by saying, "[Sally], you are not flawed. You are becoming like Christ . . ." and personalize your affirmation in your own words.

PAUSE 4_JOURNEYING FORWARD

EPHESIANS 4:1. I . . . beg you to lead a life worthy of your calling, for you have been called by God. (NLT)

How have you experienced God this week?

Select one verse or passage that was meaningful to you this week and write it here.

We live in a world of images that deeply influence how we look at life. Choose a picture from this chapter that is meaningful or disturbing to you, and briefly explain why.

Next respond to one or more of these questions in the journal on the next page. From this study is there some . . .

PROMISE from God for me to embrace?

ACTION to take?

THOUGHT about God or life to consider?

THANKFULNESS to offer?

EMOTION to express in an honest and godly way?

RELATIONSHIP to build up or reconcile?

NEED to meet?

SINFUL action or motive to confess and forsake?

JOURNAL

DIGGING DEEPER

Let's recap where we've come so far in understanding who God says we are and how it connects with your current reality. <u>Truth: What God created beautiful (that's you!) and sin marred (that's also you!), Jesus is in the process of transforming (you again!).</u> Of course we can't capture the wonder and complexity of human life in a chart. But like a prism we can try to separate out a few of the most beautiful "colors" of our new identity in Christ.

From the list earlier in Pause 3:

- **Left side:** Write a few words or phrases that describe your sense of fallen humanity.
- **Right side:** Write a few words or phrases that describe your sense of redeemed humanity.
- From everything you have discovered so far in this chapter, circle the ONE aspect of your new identity in Christ from the right side of the diagram where you would most like to experience progress. Talk with God about what that would look like for you and what it would take.

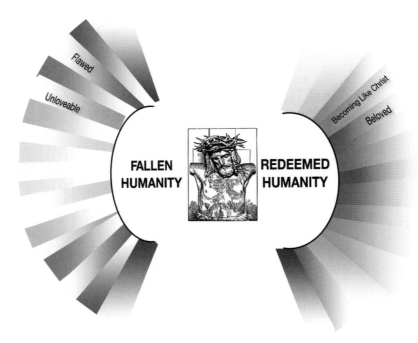

Redemption is restoring the work of God's original creation. This grace is not regarded as planting something new in essentially bad soil, but rather releasing the goodness that is in us, albeit in bondage to evil. Literally, redemption means purchasing back something that was lost, through the payment of a ransom. This is not some rational formula, nor merely a ticket to heaven; nor is it some impersonal union with the universe. We actually become a new creation in Christ. By his redemption, God sets us free from our bondage to sin and spiritual death, to be who we were originally designed to be.

— JONATHAN S. CAMPBELL WITH JENNIFER CAMPBELL, *THE WAY OF JESUS*

CHAPTER 6
MY NEW IDENTITY: WHO DOES GOD SAY I AM?

Sam knew who he was — he was an engineer, he was athletic, he was Sarah's fiancé, he was a follower of Jesus. Sam had never deeply considered the power of his identity until recently when someone had suggested that people tend to act out of who they perceive they are.

That raised a lot of questions and concerns for Sam. Like who would he be if he couldn't get a job in engineering? Or if an injury knocked him out of sports? Or if Sarah changed her mind?

Who am I?

Who decides who I am?

Who does God say that I am?

These weren't easy questions. But Sam knew that if he didn't face them, he'd probably just default to letting his friends and his culture define him.

A couple of years ago Sam met Jesus in a personal way. Jesus' call on his life offered him new ways to view himself — new relational identities. Jesus had called him to become a child of God, a disciple, a friend, and a servant. Somehow all this fit into the puzzle of his identity — Sam just wasn't sure how. But he felt a stronger desire to discover himself within his relationship with Jesus.

Furthermore, he still struggled with sin. He wondered how he could be a friend of Jesus if his life contradicted this.

PAUSE 1_EXPLORING WHAT GOD SAYS

The moral qualities which belong to the divine image were lost at the Fall; God's image in man has been universally defaced, for all mankind has in one way or another lapsed into ungodliness. But the Bible tells us that now, in ful-fillment of His plan of redemption, God is at work in Christians to repair His ruined image by communicating these qualities to them afresh. This is what Scripture means when it says that Christians are being renewed in the image of Christ (2 Corinthians 3:18) and of God (Colossians 3:10).

— J. I. PACKER, *KNOWING GOD*

To get a handle on this concept, consider these passages. Each one mentions something new that we have "in Christ" or tells something about who we are "in Christ." As you read, do two things:

1. Highlight or underline any key words or phrases that describe what is now true about us when we are "in Christ."
2. After reading the verses, stop and summarize in a few sentences what you learned about being re-created in Jesus' image and what is now true about you. (We'll get you started in Romans.)

YOUR SUMMARY:	"IN CHRIST" FROM ROMANS:
Romans says that in Christ I don't have to give sin a vote in how I live my life. Sin can't jerk me around anymore. Instead I am vibrantly alert to God, like He's present with me all the time. I don't have to feel judged or condemned because Jesus already paid for all the stuff I'm ashamed of. . . . ADD YOUR INSIGHTS:	ROMANS 6:11. In the same way, count yourselves <u>dead to sin</u> but <u>alive to God</u> in Christ Jesus. ROMANS 6:23. For the wages of sin is death, but the gift of God is <u>eternal life</u> in Christ Jesus our Lord. ROMANS 8:1. Therefore, there is now no <u>condemnation</u> for those who are in Christ Jesus. ROMANS 8:39. Neither height nor depth, <u>nor anything else in all creation</u>, will be able to <u>separate us from the love of God</u> that is in Christ Jesus our Lord. ROMANS 12:5. So in Christ we who are <u>many form one body</u>, and each member <u>belongs to all the others</u>.

"IN CHRIST" FROM EPHESIANS:	YOUR SUMMARY:
EPHESIANS 1:3. Praise be to the God and Father of our Lord Jesus Christ, who has blessed us in the heavenly realms with every spiritual blessing in Christ. EPHESIANS 2:7. In order that in the coming ages he might show the incomparable riches of his grace, expressed in his kindness to us in Christ Jesus. EPHESIANS 2:10. For we are God's workmanship, created in Christ Jesus to do good works, which God prepared in advance for us to do. EPHESIANS 4:32. Be kind and compassionate to one another, forgiving each other, just as in Christ God forgave you.	

Define yourself radically as one beloved by God. This is the true self. Every other identity is an illusion.

— JOHN EAGAN

"IN CHRIST" FROM COLOSSIANS:	YOUR SUMMARY:
COLOSSIANS 1:28. We proclaim him, admonishing and teaching everyone with all wisdom, so that we may present everyone perfect in Christ. COLOSSIANS 2:9-10. For in Christ all the fullness of the Deity lives in bodily form, and you have been given fullness in Christ, who is the head over every power and authority. COLOSSIANS 2:17. These are a shadow of the things that were to come; the reality, however, is found in Christ.	

SUMMARY: Add to the prism illustration on the next page any words and phrases from your study that describe what's true about your new identity "in Christ."

REDEEMED
HUMANITY

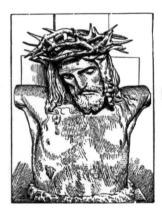

Recreated/ Being
Transformed into
the Image of
Christ

Dead to Sin

Alive to God

PAUSE 2_EXPLORING YOUR REALITY

We come to know who we are in the context of relationships — not in isolation.

Go back and replay a few of those verses you just read in Pause 1. But this time, notice how being "in Christ" influences your relationships with other people — either directly or indirectly.

Think of someone whose relationship with you is a bit strained for some reason. Try reading these verses out loud. Wherever you see a blank, put in that person's name (or "him . . . her . . . he . . . she").

> *ROMANS 8:1. Therefore, there is now no condemnation for _____ who [is] in Christ Jesus.*
>
> *EPHESIANS 2:7. In order that in the coming ages he might show the incomparable riches of his grace, expressed in his kindness to _____ in Christ Jesus.*
>
> *EPHESIANS 2:10. For _____ [is] God's workmanship, created in Christ Jesus to do good works, which God prepared in advance for _____ to do.*
>
> *1 TIMOTHY 1:14. The grace of our Lord was poured out on _____ abundantly, along with the faith and love that are in Christ Jesus.*
>
> *2 TIMOTHY 1:9. Who has saved _____ and called _____ to a holy life — not because of anything _____ [has] done but because of his [God's] own purpose and grace. This grace was given _____ in Christ Jesus before the beginning of time.*
>
> *1 PETER 5:10. And the God of all grace, who called _____ to his eternal glory in Christ, after _____ [has] suffered a little while, will himself restore _____ and make _____ strong, firm and steadfast.*
>
> *COLOSSIANS 2:9-10. For in Christ all the fullness of the Deity lives in bodily form, and _____ [has] been given fullness in Christ, who is the head over every power and authority.*

Write down how you felt as you put others' names in these verses.

How do you think viewing other people in their true identity in Christ has influenced or would influence your relationships?

[One's name] is the man's own symbol — his soul's picture, in a word — the sign which belongs to him and to no one else. Who can give a man this, his own name? God alone. For no one but God sees what the man is. . . . It is only when the man has become his name that God gives him the stone with his name upon it, for then first can he understand what his name signifies. . . . Such a name cannot be given until the man is the name . . . that being whom He had in His thought when He began to make the child, and whom He kept in His thought through the long processes of creation that went to realize the idea. To tell the name is to seal the success — to say, "In thee I am well pleased."
— GEORGE MACDONALD, *UNSPOKEN SERMONS*

Think about your name — and your various nicknames. Who gave them to you? What do they mean (if anything) to you?

PRAYER PAUSE

Have you ever sensed God calling you by an endearing name — other than the one on your driver's license? If so, describe that experience. If not, why not pause for prayer and ask Him what "name" He uses when He thinks of you.

> REVELATION 2:17. *He who has an ear, let him hear what the Spirit says to the churches. To him who overcomes, I will give some of the hidden manna. I will also give him a white stone with a new name written on it, known only to him who receives it.*

When you see God face-to-face, what new name would you like Him to call you?

PAUSE 3_COMING ALIVE TO GOD AND OTHERS

It's helpful to explore the questions "Who am I?" and "Who do others say I am?" Getting an outside opinion on our identity may help correct some of the distortion caused by our own sin and shame and limited perspective. Of course, others' answers would depend on their relationship to you. To your dad, your identity is "son" or "daughter." To your coach, your identity is "athlete." You get the picture.

But is that really your core identity? No way. By far the most critical question to ask is "Who does God say I am?" That's what we hope you'll take away from this chapter.

The Bible is full of metaphors that try to capture our identity in relation to God — such as being His child, servant, disciple, sheep, etc. No one or two of them is adequate to express everything about who we are to God. According to the Bible, if we are "in Christ," we have ALL of these identities. From God's perspective, you already are all of these things. But we don't experience them all equally or at the same time.

For example, let's explore one of our identities from creation — we are like clay in the hands of a potter.

- How do a potter and clay relate to one another?

- Summarize the key thought about our identity as clay from Isaiah 64:8.

- Using cross-references or a Bible concordance, find several other verses or passages comparing our relationship to God as clay to a potter. List the references below, and summarize the key thought in each.

- Is there anything about this biblical identity that has significant meaning to you?

- Take a moment to pray to God the Potter from your identity as clay in His hands. Write anything significant that arises from your conversation.

INSTRUCTIONS: As you study this chart, circle several aspects of your new identity (from the "You Are" column) that you identify with most. Example: potter and clay

	SINCE GOD IS . . .	YOU ARE . . .	
IDENTITIES FROM CREATION	Creator Potter Owner	Creature Clay Steward	Genesis 2:7 Isaiah 64:8 Genesis 1:26,28
IDENTITIES FROM REDEMPTION	Judge Redeemer Savior	Sinner Saint Saved	Romans 3:23 Ephesians 3:18 John 10:9
IDENTITIES OF AUTHORITY	Lord Teacher King King Head Cornerstone	Servant Disciple Citizen Ambassador Body Building	Colossians 4:7 Luke 14:27 Ephesians 2:19 2 Corinthians 5:20 Colossians 1:18 Ephesians 2:20-21
IDENTITIES OF BONDING	Father Shepherd Friend Bridegroom God	Child Sheep Friend Bride Priest	1 John 3:1 John 10:14-16 John 15:5 Ephesians 5:22-33 1 Peter 2:5

Now select one relational identity you circled above.

How do a _____ (from second column) and _____ (from third column) relate to one another?

Summarize the key thought about your identity from the verse provided.

Using cross-references or a Bible concordance, find several other related verses or passages. List the references below, and summarize the key thought in each.

What about this biblical identity has significant meaning to you?

Pray from this identity. Write anything significant that arises from your conversation with God.

If this process of meditation has been valuable for you, consider repeating it again with other aspects of your identity in relation to God that you want to explore. Use the following process to guide your meditation, writing your responses in a journal.

- How do a _____ and _____ relate to one another?
- Summarize the key thought about your identity from the verse provided.
- Using cross-references or a Bible concordance, find several other related verses or passages. List the references, and summarize the key thought in each.
- What about this biblical identity has significant meaning to you?
- Pray from this identity. Write anything significant that arises from your conversation with God.

Now take a moment to respond to
the questions in the box from Philip
Yancey.

*What would it mean if I came to the place where I saw my primary
identity in life as "the one Jesus loves"? How differently would I
view myself at the end of a day?*
— PHILIP YANCEY, *WHAT'S SO AMAZING ABOUT GRACE?*

*Deep within us, our hearts yearn to be restored, and re-story-ed, to experience again the fullness and joy of our
original blessing — to enjoy our sacred standing as image bearers of God and co-creators with him. God placed these
deep desires within our hearts as a living invitation to return to him. They evidence our humanity. They define us,
shape us, and invite us to move back to center.*
— JONATHAN S. CAMPBELL WITH JENNIFER CAMPBELL, *THE WAY OF JESUS*

Part of our human reality is that we live in time. So we cannot go back and rewrite the story
of our past. But God is in the business of shaping our future. What is one deep desire of
yours about how you want God to re-story your identity in the future?

Ultimately, it is God and God alone who defines who we truly are. If we looked up your
name in the "dictionary" of God's heart, how do you think God would define you today?

PRAYER PAUSE_ALONE

Take time to pray. Sit with God in silent worship for a while. Ask Him how He wants to relate to you at this stage of your spiritual journey . . .

- as your Father?
- as your Lord?
- as your Redeemer?
- as your Friend?
- as your Bridegroom?
- as something else?

Ask Him to deepen your intimacy with Him beyond your wildest imagination over the next twelve months, in light of this marvelous truth:

> *EPHESIANS 3:20. Now all glory to God, who is able, through his mighty power at work within us, to accomplish infinitely more than we might ask or think.* (NLT)

In light of everything Christ did to rescue and redeem you and share with you His identity as a beloved Son, take time to express your appreciation to Him now.

GROUP AFFIRMATION

Close your group time by revisiting the verses in Pause 2. Use any of these verses to affirm the other members of your group out loud.

PAUSE 4_JOURNEYING FORWARD

EPHESIANS 4:1. I . . . beg you to lead a life worthy of your calling, for you have been called by God. (NLT)

How have you experienced God this week?

Select one verse or passage that was meaningful to you this week and write it here.

We live in a world of images that deeply influence how we look at life. Choose a picture from this chapter that is meaningful or disturbing to you, and briefly explain why.

Next respond to one or more of these questions in the journal on the next page. From this study is there some . . .

PROMISE from God for me to embrace?

ACTION to take?

THOUGHT about God or life to consider?

THANKFULNESS to offer?

EMOTION to express in an honest and godly way?

RELATIONSHIP to build up or reconcile?

NEED to meet?

SINFUL action or motive to confess and forsake?

JOURNAL

SUGGESTED MEMORY VERSE:

LIKE JESUS — 1 JOHN 3:2

Dear friends, now we are children of God, and what we will be has not yet been made known. But we know that when he appears, we shall be like him, for we shall see him as he is.

CHAPTER 7
SPIRITUAL GIFTS: WHAT ARE THEY FOR?

KATHERINE'S face becomes radiant when she talks about the people she takes care of in the nursing home. It gives her genuine joy when she gets to bathe elderly patients and scrub the dead skin and dirt off their backs so they feel clean and fresh.

CHEN is a popular Bible teacher and preacher. He spells stress A-D-M-I-N-I-S-T-R-A-T-I-O-N! But sometimes he can't even go to bed on Saturday nights because he is so excited about getting to teach the next morning.

DANIEL enjoys organizing the guys in his youth group to collect twenty-five worn-out bicycles. They are fixing them up to give them to needy kids in a nearby housing project for Christmas.

ANDREA has a deep understanding of the things of God. She loves researching various cultures and social trends and then turning her insights into relevant new resources for others to use in ministry.

PAUSE 1_EXPLORING WHAT GOD SAYS

When we become God's children, rather than losing all sense of who we are, the fog begins to lift. We are more ourselves than ever. God is not interested in cranking out a bland band of followers with some cosmic cookie cutter. He who creates each single snowflake different from every other snowflake takes particular care with those created in His very image. His plan draws from the uniqueness of each person in ways that can build a supernatural unity among His incredibly diverse people.

People are mysterious, and no two of us are identical. God enjoys diversity! That's why He designed each person with different natural abilities.

What would you say are some of your strengths, skills, and natural abilities?

What would others who know you probably add to your list? (Don't worry. You're not bragging to list these. You are glorifying the God who gave them to you.)

But God does more than just give you your natural abilities. Now that His Spirit is living in you, get ready to start discovering unique ways He expresses Himself through you. This enables you to do more than you ever could naturally. The Bible refers to these expressions as spiritual gifts. Spiritual gifts are special abilities God distributes among us for the purpose of building up His people and furthering His redemptive plan.

What do you think is the difference between a natural ability and a spiritual gift?

We'll take a look at our unique design through the lens of spiritual gifts to discover how they can bless us and others for God's glory. One thing really awesome about spiritual gifts is how they enable us to experience God. But they are not primarily for our own benefit. Read through the following verses and consider why God gives spiritual gifts to His children.

WHY GOD GIVES US SPIRITUAL GIFTS:

ROMANS 12:4-5. *Just as our bodies have many parts and each part has a special function, so it is with Christ's body. We are many parts of one body, and we all belong to each other.* (NLT)

1 CORINTHIANS 12:7,24-26. *A spiritual gift is given to each of us so we can help each other. . . . God has put the body together such that extra honor and care are given to those parts that have less dignity. This makes for harmony among the members, so that all the members care for each other. If one part suffers, all the parts suffer with it, and if one part is honored, all the parts are glad.* (NLT)

EPHESIANS 4:12-16. *Their responsibility is to equip God's people to do his work and build up the church, the body of Christ. This will continue until we all come to such unity in our faith and knowledge of God's Son that we will be mature in the Lord, measuring up to the full and complete standard of Christ. Then we will no longer be immature like children. We won't be tossed and blown about by every wind of new teaching. . . . Instead, we will speak the truth in love, growing in every way more and more like Christ, who is the head of his body, the church. He makes the whole body fit together perfectly. As each part does its own special work, it helps the other parts grow, so that the whole body is healthy and growing and full of love.* (NLT)

1 PETER 4:10-11. *God has given each of you a gift from his great variety of spiritual gifts. Use them well to serve one another. . . . Then everything you do will bring glory to God through Jesus Christ. All glory and power to him forever and ever! Amen.* (NLT)

Try to summarize what you learned about the purposes and desired results of spiritual gifts.

Two Greek words are translated as "spiritual gifts" in the New Testament. One of them is <u>pneumatikos</u>, which literally means "spirituals." The other word is <u>charisma</u>, which means "a bestowment of grace." Paul uses both to describe what the Holy Spirit brings to every person whose heart He enters.

> *1 CORINTHIANS 12:1,4. Now about spiritual gifts [pneumatikos], brothers, I do not want you to be ignorant. . . . There are different kinds of gifts [charisma], but the same Spirit.*

What do you think is "spiritual" (pneumatikos) about spiritual gifts? Try to brainstorm several responses.

GRACE: God's favor, mercy, and blessings given to us just because He wants to — not because we deserve them in any way.

What does grace have to do with spiritual gifts? Write your observations in the margin.

> *ROMANS 12:3,6. For by the <u>grace</u> given me I say to every one of you: Do not think of yourself more highly than you ought [about your spiritual gifts]. . . . We have different gifts, according to the <u>grace</u> given us.*

> *1 PETER 4:10. Each one should use whatever gift he has received to serve others, faithfully administering <u>God's grace</u> in its various forms.*

Of course, the Holy Spirit brings lots of other things into our lives besides spiritual gifts.

> GALATIANS 5:22-23,25. *But the fruit of the Spirit is love, joy, peace, patience, kindness, goodness, faithfulness, gentleness and self-control. Against such things there is no law. . . . Since we live by the Spirit, let us keep in step with the Spirit.*

Why do you think these qualities are called "fruit" of the Spirit?

What connection, if any, might the fruit of the Spirit have with the spiritual gifts the Holy Spirit gives?

113

PAUSE 2 _ EXPLORING YOUR REALITY

A TRUE STORY: Eric Liddell was a Scottish sprinter who qualified to compete in the 1924 Olympics. But to train, he had to stop his studies in theology. His sister Jennie felt he shouldn't let anything delay his preparation for the mission field. He was really torn over what he should do. What finally convinced him to compete was his conviction:

> "I believe God made me for a purpose, but He also made me fast. And when I run, I feel His pleasure. To give it up would be to hold Him in contempt; to win is to honor Him."

He not only won the gold medal, but he set a world record in the 400-meter race that stood for more than a decade. After the Olympics, he finished his theological studies, became a missionary in China, and eventually died in a Japanese prison camp just weeks before American troops liberated the camp in 1945. (To learn more about Eric Liddell, view the movie *Chariots of Fire*.)

From whatever you know about him, what were probably some of Eric Liddell's passions, abilities, burdens, and spiritual gifts? How did they merge to bring glory to God?

When you consider the way God made you, including your abilities and passions, what are you doing when you genuinely feel His pleasure? (Warning: Not everything that pleases you also pleases God.)

How might pursuing that activity or developing that ability bring honor to God?

> *There is a desire within each of us, in the deep center of ourselves that we call our heart. We were born with it, it is never completely satisfied, and it never dies. We are often unaware of it, but it is always awake. . . . Our true identity, our reason for being, is to be found in this desire.*
>
> — GERALD MAY, *THE AWAKENED HEART*

Is there some desire, passion, or dream in your heart, flowing from your true identity, that gives you a reason for being? If so, describe it.

REALITY CHECK:

Spiritual transformation is a dynamic process along a lifetime journey. So is the exercising of your spiritual gift(s). Don't expect to nail down your gift(s) and develop it and exercise it — all by the time you're twenty-one. In early adulthood it's appropriate to do these three simple things:

1. Pay attention to what motivates you in serving God. What desires are bubbling inside? Notice what you're doing when you "feel God's pleasure."
2. Get lots of different experiences. Experiment. Try. Take a risk. Do things outside your comfort zone.

3. Then, listen for the affirmation of others, because you are probably not the best person to identify your own potential or emerging spiritual gifts. When you want more clarity, ask a friend or spiritual mentor how they have seen God consistently blessing others through you.

When the three come together frequently over time (i.e., what really motivates you also really blesses others), you're probably getting close to identifying your spiritual gift.

PAUSE 3_COMING ALIVE TO GOD AND OTHERS

Let's see what spiritual gifts actually looked like when people were exercising them. Here is a list of some spiritual gifts mentioned in the Bible. If you aren't sure what they mean, consult the descriptions on the next page. Try to match these characters with the spiritual gift(s) they were probably contributing. (For some, there can be more than one answer.)

_____ All of the disciples (ACTS 2:1-4)

_____ Peter (ACTS 2:14-41, especially 37-41)

_____ Peter (ACTS 3:6-7)

_____ Steven and six others (ACTS 6:1-6)

_____ Philip (ACTS 8:26-35)

_____ Tabitha (ACTS 9:36)

_____ Barnabas (ACTS 11:22-24)

_____ Saul and Barnabas (ACTS 13:1-5)

_____ Saul and Barnabas (ACTS 13:6-12)

_____ Apollos (ACTS 18:24-28)

_____ Priscilla and Aquila (ACTS 18:24-28)

_____ (your choice) _____

SPIRITUAL GIFTS:

a. Teaching
b. Wisdom
c. Serving/Able to help others
d. Prophecy
e. Mercy, helping the poor
f. Apostle
g. Evangelist
h. Leadership
i. Miraculous powers
j. Knowledge
k. Healing
l. Faith
m. Distinguishing between spirits
n. Tongues
o. Encouragement
p. Other? _____

After reading these stories, what other observations or questions do you have about spiritual gifts?

Now, try to identify what spiritual gifts may look like when exercised today. List three mature believers you know. List their names and describe what they did that built up the body of Christ or advanced God's kingdom in some way. Which spiritual gift(s) might each person have been using? How did they bless you?

SPIRITUAL GIFTS SUMMARY

(Adapted from Ralph Ennis, Breakthru: Discovering My Spiritual Gifts)

GIFT	FUNCTION	DEFINITION
ADMINISTRATION	Managing, organizing	Ability to manage and organize people, information, and things to work efficiently in the body of Christ.
APOSTLE	Initiating	Ability to see the overall picture of how the purposes of God can be furthered and to provide what is needed or lacking.
DISCERNING SPIRITS	Evaluating, sensitivity	Ability to perceive whether a person ministering in God's name really has their source from God, Satan, or human power.
EVANGELIST	Recruiting	Ability and drive to communicate with boldness and confidence the good news of Jesus Christ to those who are not believers.
EXHORTATION	Counseling, motivation	Ability to comfort, encourage, confront, challenge, and instruct others by motivating and guiding toward truth.
FAITH	Initiating, believing	Ability to believe God with extraordinary confidence for changes and spiritual growth, knowing that God will fulfill His purposes in every situation.
GIVING	Resourcing needs	Ability to determine the needs of people and provide financial or other resources to help meet those needs.
HEALING	Physical healing	Ability to call upon God to heal the sick supernaturally, demonstrating the power and glory of God.
HELPS	Detailed implementing	Ability to work alongside another and help that person complete the tasks and use the spiritual gifts God gave them.
INTERPRETATION	Interpreting tongues	Ability to understand and communicate the meaning of an unknown language spoken by someone with the gift of tongues.
KNOWLEDGE	Understanding	Ability to seek out, remember, and make effective use of a variety of information on a number of diverse subjects.

GIFT (con't)	FUNCTION (con't)	DEFINITION (con't)
MERCY	Relieving emotional hurt	Ability to perceive the hurts of others who suffer with great empathy and compassion and consoling them without condemnation.
MIRACLES	Authenticating	Ability to call upon God to do supernatural acts that cause others to consider God's will for their lives.
PASTOR/SHEPHERD	Spiritual caring	Ability to care for, feed, guide, and protect the long-term spiritual needs of people and oversee their growth in Christ.
PROPHECY	Recognition, proclamation, quality control	Ability to boldly recognize errors and sinful behavior and a driving compulsion to confront others, proclaiming God's truth related to the present and future.
RULING/LEADERSHIP	Managing, organizing	Ability to provide overall vision and direction to do God's work while coordinating efforts so that others willingly follow and work together.
SERVING	Meeting practical, physical needs	Ability to identify and use whatever resources necessary to meet the practical needs of others.
TEACHING	Communicate and illustrate truth	Ability to understand and accurately communicate the truth of God in a clear and relevant manner so that people learn.
TONGUES	Authoritative Word in certain contexts	Ability to speak a language, known or unknown, without prior knowledge of that language.
WISDOM	Practical application	Ability to discern and counsel others with applicable principles and knowledge from God's Word for complex situations.

PRAYER PAUSE_TOGETHER

Close by thanking God for bringing other gifted people into your life to help you mature.

PAUJE 4_JOURNEYING FORWARD

EPHESIANS 4:1. I . . . beg you to lead a life worthy of your calling, for you have been called by God. (NLT)

How have you experienced God this week?

Select one verse or passage that was meaningful to you this week and write it here.

We live in a world of images that deeply influence how we look at life. Choose a picture from this chapter that is meaningful or disturbing to you, and briefly explain why.

Next respond to one or more of these questions in the journal on the next page. From this study is there some . . .

PROMISE from God for me to embrace?

ACTION to take?

THOUGHT about God or life to consider?

THANKFULNESS to offer?

EMOTION to express in an honest and godly way?

RELATIONSHIP to build up or reconcile?

NEED to meet?

SINFUL action or motive to confess and forsake?

JOURNAL

CHAPTER 8
SPIRITUAL GIFTS: HOW AM I DESIGNED?

To Sarah the idea of spiritual gifts really seemed more like spiritual responsibilities. And that wasn't her idea of a gift. The responsibility of teaching, of serving, or giving made sense to her. But to call these gifts seemed weird.

Over the years, since beginning to serve within her gifting, Sarah had come to embrace the paradox that to serve others is a blessing to the giver as much as to the receiver.

However, she struggled with her gifts. They seemed to be the lesser gifts. Why had God not blessed her with the greater gifts that people praise? No one seemed to publicly praise her gifts of mercy and serving. She liked gifts, but she also liked praise. Couldn't she have both?

PAUSE 1_COMING ALIVE TO GOD AND OTHERS

We are diverse because we have different gifts. Yet we are in unity because we are all part of Christ's body. Unity in diversity is at the core of understanding God's purposes for us. Study and mark these passages for principles about spiritual gifts.

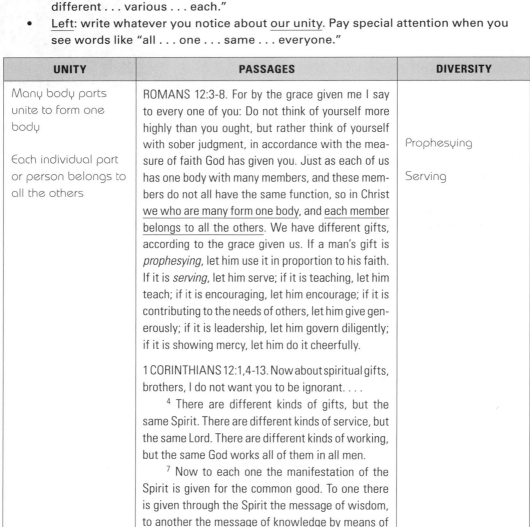

- Right: record anything you notice about the <u>diversity of gifts</u>. List any gifts mentioned. Also pay special attention when you see words like "some . . . if . . . different . . . various . . . each."
- Left: write whatever you notice about <u>our unity</u>. Pay special attention when you see words like "all . . . one . . . same . . . everyone."

UNITY	PASSAGES	DIVERSITY
Many body parts unite to form one body Each individual part or person belongs to all the others	ROMANS 12:3-8. For by the grace given me I say to every one of you: Do not think of yourself more highly than you ought, but rather think of yourself with sober judgment, in accordance with the measure of faith God has given you. Just as each of us has one body with many members, and these members do not all have the same function, so in Christ <u>we who are many form one body</u>, and <u>each member belongs to all the others</u>. We have different gifts, according to the grace given us. If a man's gift is *prophesying*, let him use it in proportion to his faith. If it is *serving*, let him serve; if it is teaching, let him teach; if it is encouraging, let him encourage; if it is contributing to the needs of others, let him give generously; if it is leadership, let him govern diligently; if it is showing mercy, let him do it cheerfully. 1 CORINTHIANS 12:1,4-13. Now about spiritual gifts, brothers, I do not want you to be ignorant. . . . ⁴ There are different kinds of gifts, but the same Spirit. There are different kinds of service, but the same Lord. There are different kinds of working, but the same God works all of them in all men. ⁷ Now to each one the manifestation of the Spirit is given for the common good. To one there is given through the Spirit the message of wisdom, to another the message of knowledge by means of	Prophesying Serving

UNITY (con't)	PASSAGES (con't)	DIVERSITY (con't)
	the same Spirit, to another faith by the same Spirit, to another gifts of healing by that one Spirit, to another miraculous powers, to another prophecy, to another distinguishing between spirits, to another speaking in different kinds of tongues, and to still another the interpretation of tongues. All these are the work of one and the same Spirit, and he gives them to each one, just as he determines. ^{12} The body is a unit, though it is made up of many parts; and though all its parts are many, they form one body. So it is with Christ. For we were all baptized by one Spirit into one body — whether Jews or Greeks, slave or free — and we were all given the one Spirit to drink. EPHESIANS 4:11-13. It was he who gave some to be apostles, some to be prophets, some to be evangelists, and some to be pastors and teachers, to prepare God's people for works of service, so that the body of Christ may be built up until we all reach unity in the faith and in the knowledge of the Son of God and become mature, attaining to the whole measure of the fullness of Christ. 1 PETER 4:10-11. Each one should use whatever gift he has received to serve others, faithfully administering God's grace in its various forms. If anyone speaks, he should do it as one speaking the very words of God. If anyone serves, he should do it with the strength God provides, so that in all things God may be praised through Jesus Christ. To him be the glory and the power for ever and ever. Amen.	

Review what you wrote in the left column. Ideally, how do our spiritual gifts express our unity in Christ?

Refer to what you wrote in the right column. Ideally, how do our spiritual gifts express our diversity in Christ?

Now that you have identified about eighteen to twenty different spiritual gifts mentioned in the Bible, don't you wonder how the Holy Spirit coordinates all of them so they work together in ministry? For fun, study the following chart to see how the gifts you listed above might be grouped into four primary contributions — depending on whether they focus on expanding, equipping, serving, or guiding others. (Some gifts might fit in more than one group.) There are other ways to "group" the spiritual gifts.

A MODEL OF HOW GIFTS WORK IN MINISTRY

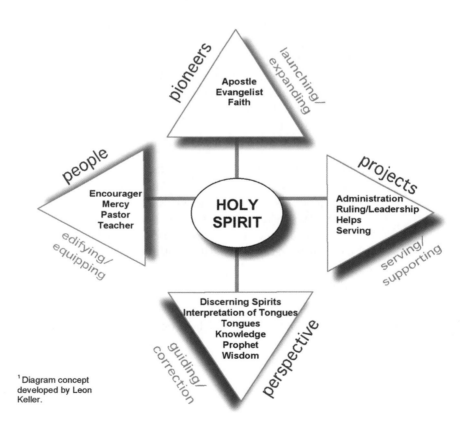

[1] Diagram concept developed by Leon Keller.

Remember how God created us in His image — and it was "very good" — at least until we messed it up by our sinful choices? Well, the same can be true of the spiritual gifts that God gives us. If there is a way to sideline, misuse, abuse, show off, profit from, or fake a spiritual gift, you can be sure someone has done it. Consider (and mark) how that might happen from this passage.

HISTORICAL BACKGROUND:
The people of Corinth had a reputation for being unruly, hard-drinking, and sexually promiscuous before they heard the gospel. As you can imagine, they didn't automatically become godly afterward; their reputations came with them into their new life in Christ. They were also very gifted people! But instead of glorifying God and promoting maturity and unity with their giftedness, it was causing all sorts of havoc and destroying their relationships. They were splintering into cliques, compromising morally, and competing over their spiritual gifts.

1 CORINTHIANS 12:14-27. Now the body is not made up of one part but of many. If the foot should say, "Because I am not a hand, I do not belong to the body," it would not for that reason cease to be part of the body. And if the ear should say, "Because I am not an eye, I do not belong to the body," it would not for that reason cease to be part of the body. If the whole body were an eye, where would the sense of hearing be? If the whole body were an ear, where would the sense of smell be? But in fact God has arranged the parts in the body, every one of them, just as he wanted them to be. If they were all one part, where would the body be? As it is, there are many parts, but one body.

21 The eye cannot say to the hand, "I don't need you!" And the head cannot say to the feet, "I don't need you!" On the contrary, those parts of the body that seem to be weaker are indispensable, and the parts that we think are less honorable we treat with special honor. And the parts that are unpresentable are treated with special modesty, while our presentable parts need no special treatment. But God has combined the members of the body and has given greater honor to the parts that lacked it, so that there should be no division in the body, but that its parts should have equal concern for each other. If one part suffers, every part suffers with it; if one part is honored, every part rejoices with it. Now you are the body of Christ, and each one of you is a part of it.

In verses 14-20, what lie did the foot and the ear buy into?

In verses 21-26, what lie did the eye and the head buy into?

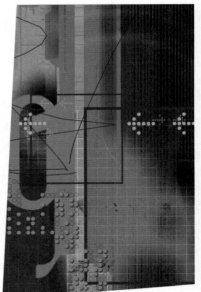

What negative consequences might happen when people believe any of these lies?

Have you ever felt like this? If so, what negative consequences occurred from believing these lies?

What are two or three points Paul makes by comparing our physical bodies to the body of Christ?

What if one of your body parts becomes diseased, or stops functioning, or is removed? What effects would the rest of your body feel?

What if believers stop contributing their spiritual gifts to the rest? How would that affect the advancement of the gospel?

Have you ever seen someone abuse a spiritual gift by doing it from the flesh, or by controlling, manipulating, or intimidating others, or by dividing a group? Explain.

Why is it crucial that any spiritual gift come under the control of the Holy Spirit?

GALATIANS 5:16. My counsel is this: Live freely, animated and motivated by God's Spirit. Then you won't feed the compulsions of selfishness. (MSG)

2 PETER 2:1. But there were also false prophets among the people, just as there will be false teachers among you. They will secretly introduce destructive heresies, even denying the sovereign Lord who bought them — bringing swift destruction on themselves.

How might God be inviting you to embrace more "grace-fully" the unique way He has designed you?

PAUSE 2_EXPLORING YOUR REALITY

When God invites us to partner with Him, He usually uses us *as we are* and *wherever we are*. He also tends to use *all that we are*. Understanding which spiritual gift you have been given may help you know what opportunities to look for. But other parts of our design may influence *where, when, how*, and *with whom* we prefer to contribute our spiritual gifts.[1]

How could your personality preferences and skills and passions and burdens complement your spiritual gifts to maximize your ministry influence?

For example, does your personality make you more comfortable with (circle your preferences):

- crowds OR small groups
- building relationships OR accomplishing tasks
- well-defined responsibilities OR launching new endeavors
- ongoing duties OR frequent changes in who, where, and why you serve
- being in charge OR supporting others who are in charge

MY PERSONALITY PREFERENCES:

Using the bulleted list above as well as other things you know about yourself, list your preferences.

---

1. Material in this Pause is adapted from "Unwrapping Your Spiritual Gifts" by Jane A. G. Kise, *Discipleship Journal*, Sep-Oct 2005.

MY SKILLS, TALENTS, AND HOBBIES:

List activities you enjoy and do well.

MY PASSIONS AND BURDENS:

List Spirit-controlled things that get you jazzed or needs that your soul responds to.

Do you receive these as responsibilities for service or as gifts that you enjoy? (Why are they called gifts instead of responsibilities?)

PAUSE 3_COMING ALIVE TO GOD AND OTHERS

IF YOU ARE UNDER TWENTY-FIVE:

For most of us, our twenties and early thirties are not years of narrow specialization. That's the time to explore many areas of life — interests, hobbies, jobs, and relationships. Frankly, it's pretty unusual to see a twenty-year-old clearly identifying and using his/her spiritual gifts. You are more likely to see several potential spiritual gifts emerging. So if you're under twenty-five or have known Jesus for less than five years, feel free to skip the next three pages. Or look at them to see what may be part of your journey down the road.

IF YOU ARE OVER TWENTY-FIVE:

On the other hand, if you are about twenty-five and have been walking with God for a while, give this exercise a try. Has God used you to meet physical needs? You may have the gift of serving. Has God used you to encourage people who are troubled in heart? You may have the gift of mercy or compassion. See where we're heading? To explore your potential emerging spiritual gifts, think of times when you were an active part of a community of believers. (Consider church, camps, small groups, campus organizations, individual relationships, etc.) Try to recall several specific incidents when something you did blessed others in God's family. Then try to figure out how God may have been using you in that incident and what spiritual gift it may have been reflecting. Here are some examples:

WHAT YOU DID . . .	MAYBE GOD USED YOU TO . . .	MAY REFLECT SPIRITUAL GIFT(S) OF . . .
Organized Fun Run to raise money for persecuted believers in China	Show mercy and compassion, help others see and respond to needs	Administration, giving, mercy, exhortation??
Stayed up all night to care for my sick roommate and pray for him	Encourage and help someone in physical need	Serving, faith, healing, encouragement??

From these incidents, do you notice any common themes that suggest how God may have used you to bless and build up others?

- Which potential gift(s) do you feel might be emerging in you?

- How do you feel about God giving you spiritual gifts at this point in your life?

How do you think your personality, skills, passions, and burdens may work together to complement your spiritual gift? (Give one example.)

One danger of talking about spiritual gifts is that our egos can get involved. It could lead to pride ("Hey, look how great my gifts are!") or to discouragement ("Hey, I'm lousy at all of these things!"). That's why Paul warns us to keep things in perspective.

ROMANS 12:3-6. For by the grace given me I say to every one of you: Do not think of yourself more highly than you ought, but rather think of yourself with sober judgment, in accordance with the measure of faith God has given you. Just as each of us has one body with many members, and these members do not all have the same function, so in Christ . . . we have different gifts, according to the grace given us.

GALATIANS 6:4-5. Each one should test his own actions. Then he can take pride in himself, without comparing himself to somebody else, for each one should carry his own load.

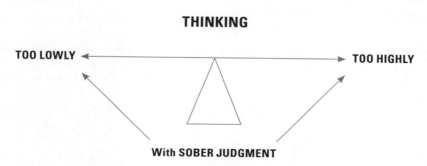

THINKING

TOO LOWLY ⟵——————————⟶ TOO HIGHLY

With **SOBER JUDGMENT**

When you think about your own spiritual gift, which way on the see-saw do you tend to lean, and how should you respond?

Consider this indispensable principle about spiritual gifts.

> *1 CORINTHIANS 12:31–13:3. And yet some of you keep competing for so-called "important" parts.*
>
> *But now I want to lay out a far better way for you.*
>
> *¹³:¹ If I speak with human eloquence and angelic ecstasy but don't love, I'm nothing but the creaking of a rusty gate.*
>
> *² If I speak God's Word with power, revealing all his mysteries and making everything plain as day, and if I have faith that says to a mountain, "Jump," and it jumps, but I don't love, I'm nothing.*
>
> *³ If I give everything I own to the poor and even go to the stake to be burned as a martyr, but I don't love, I've gotten nowhere. So, no matter what I say, what I believe, and what I do, I'm bankrupt without love.* (MSG)

Why is love necessary when we use any gift?

Think of one spiritual gift that you might have, and write it in the first blank. Now personalize the thought from 1 Corinthians 13 below:

If I have the gift of _____ ,

and can _____ ,

and can _____ ,

but do not have love for _____ ,

I am _____ .

134

CAPSULIZING SOME KEYS

Identify principles about spiritual gifts by filling in the blanks from the choices listed below.

a. Affirmed
b. Compete
c. Dormant
d. Exalt
e. Fruit
f. His kingdom

g. Identity
h. Imitate
i. Inferior/superior
j. Joy
k. Minimize
l. Obeying

m. People
n. Perspective
o. Pioneering
p. Project
q. Significance
r. Supernatural

1. Spiritual gifts remain _____ until we believe.
2. Spiritual gifts bring us _____ when exercised.
3. Spiritual gifts express God's _____ work through us.
4. Spiritual gifts are designed to expand or advance _____ .
5. Spiritual gifts usually will be _____ by others as we exercise them.
6. On my own I am helpless without God's gift of _____ .
7. On my own I am powerless without God's gift of _____ .
8. Spiritual gifts can be misused if we try to _____ someone else.
9. . . . if we try to _____ with people who have the same gift as ours.
10. . . . if we feel _____ or _____ about our gift.
11. . . . if we avoid _____ God when He asks us to do something outside our area of gifting.
12. . . . if we exercise the gifts of the Spirit without balancing them with the _____ of the Spirit.
13. . . . if we _____ people who have "flashy" gifts.
14. . . . if we _____ people who have "humble" gifts.
15. _____ gifts expand or launch new ministries and help bring people into the kingdom of God.
16. _____-focused gifts build up believers and equip them for service in God's work.
17. _____-focused gifts serve others by providing the means, resources, and systems to see that God's kingdom continues to grow and develop.
18. _____-bringing gifts ensure that what is being taught and done is done in the Spirit and in accordance with God's Word.

135

PRAYER PAUSE

Close by thanking God for His gift(s) to you and all that He has given to you and to others. Talk with Him about how He wants you to develop and contribute your gift for His glory. In your group, spend time praying for each other and for the strengths and contributions He is developing in each one of you.

If you belong to Christ, you DO have a spiritual gift — even if you don't see it yet. If you are still unclear and don't know what it is, you can be certain of what you hope for (see Hebrews 11:1). Meanwhile it's a great time to exercise faith by thanking God now for what He will reveal and develop eventually. The fundamental fact of existence is that this trust in God, this faith, is the firm foundation under everything that makes life worth living. It's our handle on what we can't see.

> *HEBREWS 11:1. Now faith is being sure of what we hope for and certain of what we do not see.*

GROUP AFFIRMATION EXERCISE (15–30 MINUTES TOGETHER)

If you are discussing this chapter with others, set aside enough time together to identify and celebrate each other's motivated desires and contributions to God's work. Be specific. Tell each other what you see in each other regarding:

- Ways you have blessed, encouraged, or served us, either directly or indirectly
- How God's Spirit has worked through you to minister to others
- What potential spiritual gifts may be emerging in you

Use this space to take notes on the feedback and affirmation you receive from others.

RESOURCES
Many good resources and assessment tools are available to help you explore your potential emerging spiritual gift(s). We recommend one resource called Breakthru: Discovering My Spiritual Gifts. *It is available through LEAD Consulting, P.O. Box 32026, Raleigh, NC 27622; phone 919-783-0354. (See www.leadconsultingusa.com.)*

Another resource called Breakthru: Discovering My Primary Roles *will help you identify the roles you are best suited for as you work with others. You can also purchase this inventory from LEAD Consulting.*

PAUSE 4_JOURNEYING FORWARD

EPHESIANS 4:1. I . . . beg you to lead a life worthy of your calling, for you have been called by God. (NLT)

How have you experienced God this week?

Select one verse or passage that was meaningful to you this week and write it here.

We live in a world of images that deeply influence how we look at life. Choose a picture from this chapter that is meaningful or disturbing to you, and briefly explain why.

Next respond to one or more of these questions in the journal on the next page. From this study is there some . . .

PROMISE from God for me to embrace?

ACTION to take?

THOUGHT about God or life to consider?

THANKFULNESS to offer?

EMOTION to express in an honest and godly way?

RELATIONSHIP to build up or reconcile?

NEED to meet?

SINFUL action or motive to confess and forsake?

JOURNAL

SUGGESTED MEMORY VERSE:

SPIRITUAL GIFTS — 1 PETER 4:10

Each one should use whatever gift he has received to serve others, faithfully administering God's grace in its various forms.

CHAPTER 9
MEANING IN LIFE: CAN I FIND SOME?

Juan started talking to himself when the alarm went off. Why was it so hard getting motivated to get out of bed?

With a degree in information technology, he had many opportunities before him. Financially he was on the right path. Things were going well with his girlfriend. And his supervisor had suggested that in a year or two he would have influence in shaping the research agenda of the company. So why did it always feel like something was missing? Some crucial driving force was absent.

"Why am I working so hard—what good is it? What's the big picture here? Will these unanswered questions impact my future marriage? What's the meaning of it all?" These questions nagged him.

In addition, he feared squandering his opportunities because he was clueless about these foundational questions. It was not a pretty picture on the inside.

Without coming to any insights or resolution, Juan sighed, crawled out from underneath the covers, and got ready for work again.

In despair, Shakespeare's Macbeth describes life as "a tale told by an idiot, full of sound and fury, signifying nothing." Have you ever felt this way about your life?

PAUSE 1_EXPLORING WHAT GOD SAYS

So far we've discovered that our true identity — who God says we are — gives us meaning and dignity totally apart from anything we do or don't do. But there is additional meaning to be found in what we do with all we've been given. It's one thing to appreciate everything God has rescued us from in Christ. But it's another thing to embrace what He has redeemed us for. That raises the question of meaning and purpose, and that's where we're going next.

MEANING. PURPOSE.

Two very similar words. Easy to say . . . yet loaded when personalized. We wonder, Does my life feel meaningful — or meaningless? What significant purpose am I living for?

People in every age and culture ask these questions. If you haven't grappled with them yet, don't worry; you will. Whether during a healthy time of self-evaluation or in a valley of self-condemnation, sooner or later we all wonder why we're alive.

God seems to have designed life with a sense that there is some integrated, coherent meaning to life and some purpose that we can significantly influence. At least there should be. Some people never adequately answer these questions. Others find initial answers but then seem to lose sight of them in the face of the great difficulties or simple boredoms of daily life. But one thing is certain: these questions are good to keep asking.

TAKE A POLL. E-mail a few of your friends. Ask them to complete this sentence:

"My life will have meaning if . . ."

RESPONSES:

CASE STUDY IN MEANINGLESSNESS

Before we examine what Scripture has to say about a life of meaning, let's consider the alternative — a wasted and meaningless life. King Solomon (David's son) had an international reputation as the wisest and richest man in his age. Yet nobody else in the Bible searched for meaning and truth as intently as he did. Why? In order "to penetrate the absurdity of life!" (Ecclesiastes 2:3, MSG). First he applied himself to understanding wisdom (1:17) to see if human reason might hold the key to meaning and truth. He carried out great projects and enjoyed the finest of pleasures . . . maybe sensory experience was the route to meaning. Then he wrote a whole book about his discoveries.

ECCLESIASTES 1:12-17. Call me "the Quester." I've been king over Israel in Jerusalem. I looked most carefully into everything, searched out all that is done on this earth. And let me tell you, there's not much to write home about. God hasn't made it easy for us. I've seen it all and it's nothing but smoke — smoke, and spitting into the wind. Life's a corkscrew that can't be straightened, a minus that won't add up. I said to myself, "I know more and I'm wiser than anyone before me in Jerusalem. I've stockpiled wisdom and knowledge." What I've finally concluded is that so-called wisdom and knowledge are mindless and witless — nothing but spitting into the wind. (MSG)

In his book, Solomon identifies several things that promise everything, but deliver nothing. They're not bad things. But by themselves, or as an ultimate reason for living, they are meaningless and just don't satisfy the human heart. Check out these verses from Ecclesiastes and summarize what things Solomon found so empty.

2:15-16   *human wisdom and intelligence*

2:19-21

2:26

4:4

4:8

4:16

5:10

6:9

7:4

8:10,14

From your experience

Solomon's search for meaning concluded this way:

> ECCLESIASTES 12:13-14. *Now all has been heard; here is the conclusion of the matter: Fear God and keep his commandments, for this is the whole [duty] of man. For God will bring every deed into judgment, including every hidden thing, whether it is good or evil.*

[God] did not make Adam and Eve obey him. He took a risk. A staggering risk, with staggering consequences. He let others into his story, and he lets their choices shape it profoundly.

— JOHN ELDREDGE, *WILD AT HEART*

After reading these verses, what do you think about the question, "meaning in life — can I find some?"

How do you feel about the possibility of God letting you into His story and shaping its outcome — right where you are now in life? If He were to do that, how might it impact your sense of meaning in life?

Read these passages about the long-term meaning of the little things we do in daily life.

> GALATIANS 6:7-10. *Do not be deceived: God cannot be mocked. A man reaps what he sows. The one who sows to please his sinful nature, from that nature will reap destruction; the one who sows to please the Spirit, from the Spirit will reap eternal life. Let us not become weary in doing good, for at the proper time we will reap a harvest if we do not give up. Therefore, as we have opportunity, let us do good to all people, especially to those who belong to the family of believers.*

> MATTHEW 25:31-46. (Look up on your own)

According to these passages, when we look back on our lives from the perspective of eternity, what meaning will we find in the little things we did in life — or failed to do?

How do you feel about having consequences a year from now for choices you make today?

What about consequences for eternity flowing from your choices?

PAUSE 2_EXPLORING YOUR REALITY

In your observation what are some things people do or acquire to give meaning to their lives?

Have you ever felt meaningless? Why?

How did that affect your daily life?

You've already discovered what Solomon found meaningless. So what about you? Finish these two sentences as many ways as you want:

MY LIFE WILL BE MEANINGFUL IF . . .	MY LIFE WILL BE WASTED IF . . .

Three people were laying bricks. An observer went up to each one and asked the same simple question: "What are you doing?"

The first one grumbled, "Can't you see I am laying bricks?"

The second said, "As you can see, I am building a wall."

The third one said with a sweep of his arm and a brimming smile, "I know you can't see it yet, but I am creating a marvelous cathedral!"

— AUTHOR UNKNOWN, STORY TOLD IN VARIOUS FORMS

What do you think is the moral of this story? (Brainstorm several options.)

All three men were doing the same simple task. So why did the third man have such a motivating perspective on meaning and purpose?

Identify something ordinary that you do . . . like go to English class, pour coffee, drive a tank, change diapers, review a profit-loss statement, whatever. If an observer asked you "What are you doing?" how would you answer on three different levels as in the story?

Can't you see I am . . .

As you can see, I am . . .

I know you can't see it yet, but I am . . .

145

What does one's viewpoint of "seeing" have to do with experiencing meaning?

God is also building something extraordinary and eternal. When completed, it will be His masterpiece. And there is no unemployment in God's kingdom. From these verses, make observations about His work and the part He invites you to play in it.

EPHESIANS 2:20-22

1 PETER 2:5

REALITY CHECK

Let's be realistic. The point will never be to have life's meaning and purpose completely figured out — ever. So cut yourself some slack. If you find meaning and purpose in the small events of your daily life now, they will build together to a meaningful life in the long run. If your life is like a building under construction, think of your twenties as the time to lay the foundation and just rough out the frame.

This process continues through life. As we look back, we'll see what God was building through us while we served Him in faithfulness and worship.

Consider Paul's purposes for you. <u>Mark</u> the key ideas.

1 CORINTHIANS 3:11-15. For no one can lay any foundation other than the one already laid, which is Jesus Christ. If any man builds on this foundation using gold, silver, costly stones, wood, hay or straw, his work will be shown for what it is, because the Day will bring it to light. It will be revealed with fire, and the fire will test the quality of each man's work. If what he has built survives, he will receive his reward. If it is burned up, he will suffer loss; he himself will be saved, but only as one escaping through the flames.

Imagine a "building inspector" coming to inspect your life. How solid is your foundation (on Jesus Christ)?

What are the building bricks of your life? What would you like the whole "cathedral" of your life to look like when it's all put together?

What happens when gold, silver, and jewels versus wood, hay, and straw are subjected to fire? What does this imply about lasting meaning?

What is happening in your life now that could be described as "gold, silver, and jewels" or as "wood, hay, or straw"? Where will this lead?

Humans cannot easily sustain a world that's entirely random and plotless. . . . A French philosopher said, "We are condemned to meaning." There's an almost universal impulse to endow our joys and our sorrows, and our failures and our successes, with meaning.

— MARTIN MARTY

If you can, describe how one joy or success in your life became meaningful to you or taught something valuable.

Now do the same with one sorrow or failure in your life.

If a twelve-year-old you know asked you about the meaning and purpose of life, how would you explain it in simple words?

PAUSE 3_COMING ALIVE TO GOD AND OTHERS

FROM SUCCESS . . . TO SIGNIFICANCE . . . TO MEANING

Talk about the good life — King Solomon had it all. He completed amazing projects like mansions, parks, reservoirs, and temples. He was known around the world of his day for his amazing wisdom (see Proverbs — he wrote many of them), his compassionate acts, and his extravagant pleasures. But pile all these "significant" pieces together and hit "calculate." To Solomon, it all added up to a big zero — meaningless!

What about us? We arrived on planet Earth naked — and we'll leave it taking nothing with us. Memories of our existence will fade quickly. Our earthly successes vanish or are surpassed by others. Frankly, we can feel successful and significant and yet fail to grasp a deep sense of meaning in life. That's often our dilemma.

One response to this dilemma, in some circles of believers, starts by pointing out that only two things are eternal: The souls of people and God's Word. So the thinking goes that if you want your life to matter long-term, quit your job so you can go into full-time ministry connecting people with the Word of God. If God leads you to do this, that's great.

But this view leaves the impression that normal work out there in society is somehow less significant, second rate, or even "godless." Why exhaust yourself meeting people's earthly needs when you could be helping them with their spiritual needs? Before you know it, life gets cut into competing pieces, with spiritual versus material, sacred versus secular, eternal versus temporal.

There's only one problem with this view: Jesus was a carpenter for the first thirty years of His life, and Paul worked on and off as a tentmaker. Were those years "wasted" in "secular, godless, meaningless" activity? I don't think so.

Solomon's book is a guidebook for anybody in search of meaning. So what did the king who had it all and did it all discover during his lifelong search for meaning? He devoted twelve chapters to telling us all the things he had tried that had let him down. In a nutshell, he concluded, "Been there, done that, and it's all meaningless!" . . . except for two things.

In the end, Solomon's conclusion boiled down to two life principles:

ECCLESIASTES 12:13-14. Here now is my final conclusion: Fear God and obey his commands, for this is everyone's duty. God will judge us for everything we do, including every secret thing, whether good or bad. (NLT)

That's it. No explanations. Just these two verses from Solomon to help us get our hands around the meaning of life.

From verse 13, our first life purpose is to "fear God." That's worship . . . coming home to Him and remaining in His presence in awe and reverence and trust. Our second purpose is to "keep his commandments." That's faithfulness. We are called to cultivate a life of worship in all we do from carpentry to preaching, as Jesus did. And day by day we are called to live out faithfully the ways of God in our relationships — with love, mercy, grace, truth, trust, justice, holiness, etc. Simple, yet profound. As we follow God in all aspects of our lives, He brings meaning and purpose with Him into absolutely everything in our lives.

And that's not all. Verse 14 moves us into eternity. No discussion of the meaning of life can avoid the fact that someday each of us will walk through the gate called Death into eternity. We can pursue meaning in this life. But if it doesn't also extend into the life beyond, then life is meaningless in light of eternity.

Remember that God will judge "every secret thing, whether good or bad." All our hopes for lasting meaning are found there. Maybe it feels strange to you to find hope in being judged. But just consider the alternative:

What if there never is any judgment for what we humans do on this earth?

What if all that we do has no impact or any consequence whatsoever in eternity?

What if everybody just gets away with everything they've ever done — or failed to do?

How meaningless is that? Hey, we might as well just eat, drink, be merry, and die — if nothing we do will last on a planet with a dying sun and the short memories of people and the constant jockeying for power.

We're not talking about the "great white throne judgment" where the sheep will be separated from the goats to determine their eternal destiny — either heaven or hell. We mean the judgment described in 2 Corinthians 5:10.

For we must all appear before the judgment seat of Christ, that each one may receive what is due him for the things done while in the body, whether good or bad.

Now that's encouraging! Whatever we do "while in the body" actually matters to God. It all matters. The "things" we work with will all perish — the buildings, cars, computers, money, universities, pots and pans. But ALL our work will have an impact in eternity — for good or bad. There is a cause-and-effect relationship that will extend into eternity.

The apostle Paul looked forward to what awaits us in heaven.

2 TIMOTHY 4:8. Now there is in store for me the crown of righteousness, which the Lord, the righteous Judge, will award to me on that day — and not only to me, but also to all who have longed for his appearing.

Even the tedious work of a slave matters if it is done "as unto the Lord," Paul reminded the many enslaved believers of his day. If you feel chained to your job, take heart. The Lord will assign eternal consequences to whatever you do, which adorns this life with meaning.

Are you a carpenter, a parent, a businessman, a student, a highway worker, a stockbroker, an artist, or a minister? All have equal access to meaning through a life of faithful worship in all we do, think, and are.

COLOSSIANS 3:23-24. Whatever you do, work at it with all your heart, as working for the Lord, not for men, since you know that you will receive an inheritance from the Lord as a reward.

Comment on one idea that encouraged you from the previous article. Or comment on one idea that disturbed you or that you disagree with.

The Bible claims that our lives have repercussions in eternity. How do you feel about eternal consequences for all you do?

Consider the alternative. How would you feel in a world without any consequences — now or later? In other words, what if our choices here just don't matter? What would be some of the implications?

What is something big enough and significant enough that you could see yourself giving your whole life to it? How do you think that might connect with what God is doing in the world?

Try writing your own song or poem expressing your current questions and tentative answers about your life's meaning and/or purpose.

PRAYER PAUSE

Psalm 16 and Psalm 91 are both "big picture" psalms. Each of them assures us that we don't have to worry or be anxious about the future because God is in control and will work His purposes out in His own time — for your individual life and for the whole world. Take some time to read one of these psalms together prayerfully and meditatively as a group.

PAUSE 4_JOURNEYING FORWARD

EPHESIANS 4:1. I . . . beg you to lead a life worthy of your calling, for you have been called by God. (NLT)

How have you experienced God this week?

Select one verse or passage that was meaningful to you this week and write it here.

We live in a world of images that deeply influence how we look at life. Choose a picture from this chapter that is meaningful or disturbing to you, and briefly explain why.

Next respond to one or more of these questions in the journal on the next page. From this study is there some . . .

PROMISE from God for me to embrace?

ACTION to take?

THOUGHT about God or life to consider?

THANKFULNESS to offer?

EMOTION to express in an honest and godly way?

RELATIONSHIP to build up or reconcile?

NEED to meet?

SINFUL action or motive to confess and forsake?

JOURNAL

SUGGESTED MEMORY VERSE

MEANING IN LIFE — ECCLESIASTES 12:13-14

*Now all has been heard; here is the conclusion of the matter: Fear God and keep his command-
ments, for this is the whole duty of man. For God will bring every deed into judgment, including
every hidden thing, whether it is good or evil.*

154

DIGGING DEEPER: A RESOURCE ON MEANING

If you want to dig deeper into this search for meaning, if you enjoy images and interesting dialogue, here's a great resource that we encourage you to buy. It's a set of photographic images called Searching the Ordinary for Meanings.

SEARCHING THE ORDINARY FOR MEANINGS

by Ralph Ennis
(Available from NavPress at www.NavPress.com)

The phone rings, your paper is coming due, the boss demands, the bus is late, the lines get longer, the dinner burns, a child is born, guests laugh, grandmother dies, the car needs gas, the stock market soars and tumbles, the world goes on.

What does it all mean?

Through the medium of photographic images this resource looks at many ordinary actions, objects, and ideas that we all experience through life — things like clothes and childhood and play and work and sex. They ask, "What do these daily pursuits and fragmented images actually mean?" What significance do they convey that is not directly expressed? Not their functions or their utilitarian purposes or what they are for — but their meanings and what they reveal about reality. And if we dig a bit deeper, we may glimpse what they imply about God. Each topic is illustrated with pictures from ordinary life, and framed with quotations from Jesus and His followers.

Here are some of the 38 topics included:
Clothes
Work
Family
Beauty
Pain
Childhood
Sleep

Take clothes, for instance. A quick glance tells us that clothes function to protect us from the elements. But a deeper look reveals that clothes protect us from the acute embarrassment of nakedness. We realize that one significant meaning of clothes (not the only meaning, of course) is that human beings, unlike other animals, have shame.

We hope these cards will encourage and prompt you as you continue humankind's ancient search for meaning amidst the fragments of the modern life we all experience.

CHAPTER 10
LIFE'S PURPOSE: WHY AM I ALIVE?

Work was consuming. But to Bryan, finding direction in life was a bigger problem. He grew up in a home with the stresses of having little money, so working to make lots of money made sense. What didn't make sense was the purpose of living.

Bryan intuitively knew that his relationship with God should influence his daily sense of direction. It just didn't most days. And most of his friends didn't seem to have a real purpose in the things they did. "Why has God left us on earth when He could take us to heaven? What direction should my life take and how can I decide?" These questions bothered Bryan some days but not every day. Usually he just wanted to make money and have fun.

Here is a truth that reaches into the deepest part of what it means to be a person . . . that we are made to "have dominion" within an appropriate domain of reality. This is the core of the likeness or image of God in us and is the basis of the destiny for which we were formed. We are, all of us, never-ceasing spiritual beings with a unique eternal calling to count for good in God's great universe. . . . In creating human beings, God made them to rule, to reign, to have dominion in a limited sphere. Only so can they be persons.

— DALLAS WILLARD, *THE DIVINE CONSPIRACY*

PAUSE 1_EXPLORING WHAT GOD SAYS

So far we've discovered that the dignity we share with all humans comes from being created in God's image. And for believers, being transformed into Jesus' image gives us hope. Next we explored how our unique design (strengths, gifts, etc.) can make a difference in other people's lives and spiritual journeys. Then we tried to get our hands around the awesome reality that our lives have intrinsic meaning and significance because God is weaving each of our individual stories into His grand and cosmic story of redemption into eternity. In this last chapter we are exploring the bigger purposes for which God put us on this planet at this moment in time. Where we're headed is a journey toward . . .

Dignity & Hope ———► Meaning & Significance ———► Purpose & Goals ———► Destiny

Let's explore how several men and women in the Bible viewed their life's purpose and meaning. They all served God, but each served in a unique way. Each had a God-designed destiny in his or her generation. This may be a bit difficult if you are not familiar with these stories. Instead of doing them all, feel free to select one or two and go more in depth by reading his or her story for background.

From whatever you know about these people, and the selected passage, <u>summarize what each person eventually saw as his or her big life purpose or destiny.</u>

JOSHUA

Joshua was Moses' right-hand man in leading the Israelites out of 430 years of slavery in Egypt. After Moses died, Joshua prepared the people who survived the Exodus to enter the Promised Land. You can study his story starting at Joshua 21. Here he warns them to remain faithful to God in the pagan territories they will soon enter and occupy.

> *JOSHUA 24:14-15. So fear the Lord and serve him wholeheartedly. Put away forever the idols your ancestors worshiped when they lived beyond the Euphrates River and in Egypt. Serve the LORD alone. But if you refuse to serve the LORD, then choose today whom you will serve. Would you prefer the gods your ancestors served beyond the Euphrates? Or will it be the gods of the Amorites in whose land you now live? But as for me and my family, we will serve the LORD.* (NLT)

JOSHUA'S PURPOSE:

ESTHER

Esther was a beautiful young Jewish woman raised by her uncle Mordecai during the time when the brutal and pagan Persian King Xerxes reigned over a huge empire, making the conquered Jewish people his subjects. Out of all the beautiful young virgins in the territory, Xerxes selected her as his queen. One of the highest nobles in the land was named Haman. He hatched a plot to persuade Xerxes to exterminate as many Jews as possible. In this passage Mordecai pleads with Queen Esther to use her influence and risk the king's wrath to save her people from the coming genocide. This story is found in the book of Esther.

> *ESTHER 4:14. If you keep quiet at a time like this, deliverance and relief for the Jews will arise from some other place, but you and your relatives will die. Who knows if perhaps you were made queen for just such a time as this?* (NLT)

ESTHER'S PURPOSE:

PAUL

Paul was raised in Asia Minor in a strict Jewish home and rose to a high rank among the Pharisees. So at first he viewed the teachings of Christ and the young movement of His followers as a serious threat to orthodox Judaism. He was responsible for persecuting many believers before he met the risen Christ and believed in Him. He was convinced that God had commissioned him to take the wonderful news of the gospel of grace out of his Jewish comfort zone to regions beyond so that Gentiles could also be saved. His story starts in Acts 9.

> *ACTS 20:24. But my life is worth nothing to me unless I use it for finishing the work assigned me by the Lord Jesus — the work of telling others the Good News about the wonderful grace of God.* (NLT)

> *EPHESIANS 3:8-9. Though I am the least deserving of all God's people, he graciously gave me the privilege of telling the Gentiles about the endless treasures available to them in Christ. I was chosen to explain to everyone this mysterious plan that God, the Creator of all things, had kept secret from the beginning.* (NLT)

PHILIPPIANS 3:10. [For my determined purpose is] that I may know Him [that I may progressively become more deeply and intimately acquainted with Him, perceiving and recognizing and understanding the wonders of His Person more strongly and more clearly], and that I may in that same way come to know the power outflowing from His resurrection [which it exerts over believers], and that I may so share His sufferings as to be continually transformed [in spirit into His likeness even] to His death. (AMP)

PAUL'S PURPOSE:

Consider these verses about God's plans and purposes for our lives.

JEREMIAH 29:11. "For I know the plans I have for you," declares the LORD, "plans to prosper you and not to harm you, plans to give you hope and a future."

ACTS 13:36. For when David had served God's purpose in his own generation, he fell asleep.

How would it feel to reach the end of your life and know that — like King David and others you studied — you had fulfilled God's purpose for you in your generation?

PAUSE 2_EXPLORING YOUR REALITY

Take a shot at trying to express the big picture by scribbling your thoughts below:

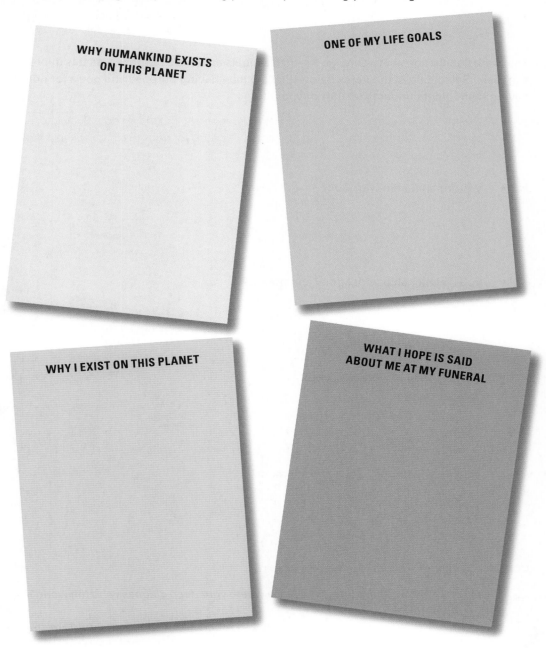

WHY HUMANKIND EXISTS ON THIS PLANET

ONE OF MY LIFE GOALS

WHY I EXIST ON THIS PLANET

WHAT I HOPE IS SAID ABOUT ME AT MY FUNERAL

There are connections between one's practical goals and one's purposes, as this quote suggests. Select one of the items below. Explain how having purpose and goals (or not having them) might impact that part of your life.

> EXAMPLE: I know that God wants me to keep my body fit, and so do I. But without specific goals that make it into my schedule, it's easy for days to slip by without exercise. My goal is to work out three times a week.

- your relationship with God?

- your relationship with family and friends?

- your attitude at work or school?

- your view of money and entertainment?

Consider Buechner's words about purpose:

> *The place where God calls you is the place where your deep gladness and the world's deep hunger meet.*
>
> — Frederick Buechner, *Wishful Thinking*

Do you have any idea where this place ("The place where God calls you") might be for you?

An environment of grace and trust gets me in touch with my destiny — which is always greater than my goals and more significant than my individual potential.

— BILL THRALL, LEADERSHIP CATALYST, INC.

Don't be worried if you don't have a clue about your destiny. Your destiny usually unfolds over time and rarely becomes clear in your twenties. In the meantime, you are not on this journey alone.

What part might other people play in helping us get in touch with our destiny?

How might others also distract or derail us?

How might God's destiny for us actually be more about others than about us?

PAUSE 3_COMING ALIVE TO GOD AND OTHERS

JOHN 17 is a great chapter to learn how Jesus viewed His sense of purpose and destiny. As you read the whole chapter in your Bible, take notes on these four questions:

WHAT PURPOSES DID JESUS BELIEVE HE HAD ACCOMPLISHED DURING HIS LIFE ON EARTH?	WHAT LIFE PURPOSES DID JESUS PASS ON TO HIS DISCIPLES? WHAT DID HE EXPECT THEM TO DO WITH THEIR LIVES AFTER HE WAS GONE?
vs. 1 — He gave glory to His Father	vss. 6-8 — to accept and keep God's Word
WHAT WERE THEY GIVEN FOR THE JOURNEY?	**WHAT WOULD THEY EXPERIENCE ON THE JOURNEY?**
vs. 13 — full measure of Jesus' joy	vs. 14 — hatred from the world

Let's not kid ourselves. Jesus' path to His destiny was difficult — very difficult. He paid a huge price in moving toward His purpose. Notice the difficulties and pain He endured from this passage:

PHILIPPIANS 2:5-11. Your attitude should be the same as that of Christ Jesus: Who, being in very nature God, did not consider equality with God something to be grasped, but made himself nothing, taking the very nature of a servant, being made in human likeness. And being found in appearance as a man, he humbled himself and became obedient to death — even death on a cross!

Therefore God exalted him to the highest place and gave him the name that is above every name, that at the name of Jesus every knee should bow, in heaven and on earth and under the earth, and every tongue confess that Jesus Christ is Lord, to the glory of God the Father.

What tough choices did Jesus make, and what did He endure on His journey toward His destiny?

Who accomplished Jesus' destiny?

What were some of the eternal consequences from Jesus' choices on earth?

Consider what the Bible has to say on the questions, "What's worth dying for?" and "What's worth living for?"

JOHN 15:12-13. This is my commandment: Love each other in the same way I have loved you. There is no greater love than to lay down one's life for one's friends. (NLT)

ROMANS 12:1. And so, dear brothers and sisters, I plead with you to give your bodies to God because of all he has done for you. Let them be a living and holy sacrifice — the kind he will find acceptable. This is truly the way to worship him. (NLT)

PHILIPPIANS 3:10-11. I want to know Christ and the power of his resurrection and the fellowship of sharing in his sufferings, becoming like him in his death, and so, somehow, to attain to the resurrection from the dead.

What might it look like for you to obey these commands in relation to other people?

Is there any purpose on earth that you would be willing to die for? Explain.

Would you be equally willing to devote your life to it? Explain.

From these words of Jesus, what should — and should not — be your primary concern? What does this mean to you?

MATTHEW 6:31-33. So don't worry about these things, saying, "What will we eat? What will we drink? What will we wear?" These things dominate the thoughts of unbelievers, but your heavenly Father already knows all your needs. Seek the Kingdom of God above all else, and live righteously, and he will give you everything you need. (NLT)

What is the cost for those who pursue God's purposes and destiny for their lives? What are some rewards?

> *JOHN 12:23-25. Jesus replied, "The hour has come for the Son of Man to be glorified. I tell you the truth, unless a kernel of wheat falls to the ground and dies, it remains only a single seed. But if it dies, it produces many seeds. The man who loves his life will lose it, while the man who hates his life in this world will keep it for eternal life."*

What might it look like for you to "lose your life" for the sake of a greater purpose or destiny?

What are some likely consequences if you try to [hold on to life just as it is (MSG)] instead?

What is the most serious temptation you face to shortchange God's purpose for you? What seems so important to you now that you might trade it for God's best plan for you?

Right now, imagine God giving you a glimpse at where "the grand drama of providence intersected the smaller scenes" of your life. What difference would that possibility make to your sense of meaning or meaninglessness?

PRAYER PAUSE

Pause to talk with God about His dreams for you. Express your heart in response to the above quote. Ask Him where you are in the journey toward fulfilling His dreams for you and how you can move forward to embrace it.

Linger awhile in His presence.

*PAUSE 4*_JOURNEYING FORWARD

EPHESIANS 4:1. I . . . beg you to lead a life worthy of your calling, for you have been called by God. (NLT)

How have you experienced God this week?

Select one verse or passage that was meaningful to you this week and write it here.

We live in a world of images that deeply influence how we look at life. Choose a picture from this chapter that is meaningful or disturbing to you, and briefly explain why.

Next respond to one or more of these questions in the journal on the next page. From this study is there some . . .

PROMISE from God for me to embrace?

ACTION to take?

THOUGHT about God or life to consider?

THANKFULNESS to offer?

EMOTION to express in an honest and godly way?

RELATIONSHIP to build up or reconcile?

NEED to meet?

SINFUL action or motive to confess and forsake?

JOURNAL

SUGGESTED MEMORY VERSE:

LIFE'S PURPOSE — PHILIPPIANS 3:10-11

I want to know Christ and the power of his resurrection and the fellowship of sharing in his sufferings, becoming like him in his death, and so, somehow, to attain to the resurrection from the dead.

DIGGING DEEPER

A PEOPLE PROJECT:

Identify one or two mature people whose lives you admire. Send them an e-mail, or better yet, give them a call or arrange for a visit. Ask these questions (and any others you think of) related to purpose and meaning in life:

- What do you think is God's big-picture purpose for your life?
- Where do you find personal meaning and significance?
- How did you discover and become convinced of your life's purpose?

THEIR RESPONSES:

CELEBRATING YOUR GROUP

As you and your group finish this study, it's a good time to celebrate together. Your relationships have deepened through these past weeks. You've learned much from each other — truths, joys, pains. So we encourage you to plan a celebration. Take some time to "Reflect Back," "Envision Forward," and "Pause to Affirm and Pray."

REFLECT BACK

Share how you've benefited from studying God's Word with this group of fellow spiritual journeyers.

How has your walk with God been affected?

How has your daily lifestyle changed?

What emotions surface as you reflect on your times together?

Somewhere deep down, we know that if we are to survive we must come together and rediscover ways to connect with each other, and with the earth that supports our collective life. We are social beings who need one another not just for physical survival but also for spiritual sustenance as we journey together. So our individuality only makes sense in the context of community, where we are free to become ourselves.
— JONATHAN S. CAMPBELL WITH JENNIFER CAMPBELL, *THE WAY OF JESUS*

ENVISION FORWARD

What are your spiritual needs as you consider the next phase of your journey?

In what environment might these needs be met?

What continuing relationships will you have with the people in this group (casual friendship to in-depth involvement)?

Are there other people you know who could benefit from studying this series?

Would it be a good stewardship of gifts for one or more people from this group to team up and facilitate a new group? Is God leading anyone to be a part of a new group?

PAUSE TO AFFIRM

Do you want to express a thank you or affirmation to anyone in the group who has influenced your life? Take time to do that.

PAUSE TO PRAY

Spend time together praying. Thank God for this part of your journey. Praise Him for who He is. Linger longer together.

WHY MEMORIZE SCRIPTURE?

You won't find the word memorize in the Bible. But the concept is there both in command and in example ("treasure . . . store up . . . hide" God's words in our hearts). We are encouraged to "study . . . reflect on . . . delight in . . . not forget" God's words (Psalm 119:9-16, NLT; 37:31).

- "lay hold of . . . pay attention . . . listen closely . . . keep [God's words] within your heart" (Proverbs 4:4,20-22).
- "bind them [my commands] around your neck . . . write them on the tablet of your heart" (Proverbs 3:3).
- "always treasure my commands. . . . Guard my instructions as you guard your own eyes. Tie them on your fingers as a reminder. . . . Write them on the tablet of your heart" (Proverbs 7:1-3, NLT, NIV).
- "it is good to keep these sayings in your heart" (Proverbs 22:18, NLT).
- "meditate on [God's words] day and night" (Joshua 1:8).

These same verses also explain the reasons for and benefits of memorizing Scripture:

- "that I might not sin against you . . . [my] feet do not slip" (Psalm 119:9-16; 37:31).
- "they bring life . . . and healing to their whole body" (Proverbs 4:22).
- "find favor with both God and people . . . earn a good reputation" (Proverbs 3:3-4, NLT).
- "you will trust in the LORD" (Proverbs 22:18-19, NLT).
- "you will be sure to obey everything written in it. Only then will you prosper and succeed" (Joshua 1:8, NLT).
- so that you'll "have all of them ready on your lips" (Proverbs 22:18).
- "your words . . . were my joy and my heart's delight" (Jeremiah 15:16).

Perhaps even more compelling than these reasons is seeing how powerfully God can use a person who has taken the time and effort to consistently memorize Scripture. When Jesus faced Satan (see Matthew 4:1-11), He drew from the many verses of Scripture that He had memorized in His youth to pinpoint Satan's deception and resist temptation. Where would we be if Jesus had not memorized Scripture? When Peter addressed the huge crowd on the day of Pentecost, he was given no time to consult his concordance and prepare a message! Because he had made Scripture memory a priority in his life, he could quote from three different Old Testament passages that helped bring 3,000 people to the Lord!

If you long to equip yourself to counteract Satan, resist sin, trust and obey God, listen to God's voice, and minister to others, there is no better investment of your time than memorizing Scripture.

A good place to begin is by revisiting the verses you memorized here in this study. Carry the verses around. Put them on your PDA. Put them on your computer. Review them out loud. Often. Write them out until you can say them accurately. Meditate on them. Pray over them. Tell a friend what they mean to you. Put yourself to sleep at night thinking about them. And look forward to listening to God speak to you!

I am amazed at the countless times God pulled from my mind a memorized verse that has been exactly the right thing at the right time! At times it was a comfort, at times guidance. A push ahead or a pull to stop. A reminder of His promise, a prompting for wisdom. A word for counseling another, an insight for those seeking our Lord.

— DENNIS STOKES

SCRIPTURE MEMORY VERSES

GOD'S GOODNESS

PSALM 34:8

Taste and see that the LORD is good; blessed is the man who takes refuge in him.

CREATED IN HIS IMAGE

GENESIS 1:27

So God created man in his own image, in the image of God he created him; male and female he created them.

ALL HAVE SINNED

ROMANS 3:23

For all have sinned and fall short of the glory of God.

MERCY FOR SIN

LAMENTATIONS 3:22-23 (NRSV)

The steadfast love of the LORD never ceases, his mercies never come to an end; they are new every morning; great is thy faithfulness.

NEW CREATION

2 CORINTHIANS 5:17

Therefore, if anyone is in Christ, he is a new creation; the old has gone, the new has come!

LIKE JESUS

1 JOHN 3:2

Dear friends, now we are children of God, and what we will be has not yet been made known. But we know that when he appears, we shall be like him, for we shall see him as he is.

SPIRITUAL GIFTS

ROMANS 12:4-6

Just as each of us has one body with many members, and these members do not all have the same function, so in Christ we who are many form one body, and each member belongs to all the others. We have different gifts, according to the grace given us.

SPIRITUAL GIFTS

1 PETER 4:10

Each one should use whatever gift he has received to serve others, faithfully administering God's grace in its various forms.

MEANING IN LIFE

ECCLESIASTES 12:13-14

Now all has been heard; here is the conclusion of the matter: Fear God and keep his commandments, for this is the whole duty of man. For God will bring every deed into judgment, including every hidden thing, whether it is good or evil.

LIFE'S PURPOSE

PHILIPPIANS 3:10-11

I want to know Christ and the power of his resurrection and the fellowship of sharing in his sufferings, becoming like him in his death, and so, somehow, to attain to the resurrection from the dead.

CONNECT SERIES OVERVIEW

CONNECT is designed to help you discover and embrace the truth Jesus spoke of in a holistic way. We long to see you enjoying life as a member of God's kingdom and family, deeply experiencing His presence, knowing His truth, resting in His love, and confident in His hope. These studies are designed to be used in small groups where people can encourage, trust, and support each other on their spiritual journeys.

CONNECT is arranged as a series of Bible studies. These studies will present foundational biblical principles for primary relationships in life. Jesus summed up what life is all about when He said, "'Love the Lord your God with all your heart and with all your soul and with all your mind.' This is the first and greatest commandment. And the second is like it: 'Love your neighbor as yourself'" (Matthew 22:37-39). Growing in your love for God, for others, and for yourself while managing your personal life in ways that honor Him — now that is a real spiritual journey!

ABOUT THE AUTHORS

RALPH ENNIS is the Director of Intercultural Training and Development for The Navigators. Ralph and his wife, Jennifer, have ministered with The Navigators since 1975 in a variety of areas, including at Norfolk military bases, Princeton University, Richmond Community, Glen Eyrie Leadership Development Institute, and with The CoMission in Moscow, Russia. Ralph has a Master's degree in Intercultural Relations. Some of his publications include *Searching the Ordinary for Meaning; Breakthru: Discover Your Spiritual Gifts and Primary Roles; Successfit: Decision Making Preferences; An Introduction to the Russian Soul;* and *The Issue of Shame in Reaching People for Christ.*

Ralph and Jennifer currently live in Raleigh, North Carolina. They have four married children and nine grandchildren.

JUDY GOMOLL is Director of School Agreements as a National Training Team Associate. Before joining The Navigators, Judy was an educator with a specialty in curriculum development. Judy and her husband, George, served with The Navigators as missionaries in Uganda and Kenya for fifteen years, where they helped pioneer ministries in communities, churches, and at Makerere University. Judy led in leader training and designing of contextualized discipleship materials and methods.

In her current role with the National Training Team, Judy is assisting in the research, development, and field testing of spiritual transformation training tools and resources. She also directs our partnerships agreements with seminaries and graduate schools.

Judy has an MA in Curriculum and Instruction, and an MA in Organizational Leadership. She and George live in Parker, Colorado.

DENNIS STOKES has been serving with The Navigators since 1973. During that time he has ministered on collegiate staff, as well as being a collegiate trainer and national training consultant. Dennis has designed, developed, and led seven summer training programs for The Navigators, and was the training coordinator for the CoMission project to the former Soviet Union. He is ordained and speaks at training events, conferences, and in church pulpits in the U.S. and twelve different countries. He also leads and participates on numerous training teams. In his role as the National Training Director for the U.S. Navigators, Dennis leads out in strategic planning, leading, and implementing national initiatives for staff training and development.

Dennis and his wife, Ellen, live in Erie, Colorado, and have three children — Christopher, Cheryl, and Amy.

CHRISTINE WEDDLE is Associate Director of National Training and Staff Development and has been on staff with The Navigators since 1997. She first connected with The Navigators when she joined the CoMission Training Team. In this role she assisted in the planning and organization of staff training events in the U.S., Russia, and the Ukraine.

Since moving to Colorado Springs in 1998, she has directed numerous national training and staff development events. She specializes in developing adult learning environments and visual resources.

Connect Even More!

The CONNECT series is designed to help you discover and embrace the truth Jesus spoke of in a holistic way. By using the series in a small group, you will find encouragement, trust, and support from others as you travel together on this spiritual journey.

God: Connecting with His Outrageous Love

Ralph Ennis, Judy Gomoll, Dennis Stokes, Christine Weddle
978-1-60006-258-2
1-60006-258-X

This study presents a foundational biblical principle for primary relationships in life: receiving God's love and loving Him in response.

Soul: Embracing My Sexuality and Emotions

Ralph Ennis, Judy Gomoll, Rebecca Goldstone, Dennis Stokes, Christine Weddle
978-1-60006-262-9
1-60006-262-8

Find out how growing in your love for God, for others, and for yourself will help manage your personal life in ways that honor Him.

Relationships: Bringing Jesus into My World

Ralph Ennis, Judy Gomoll, Rebecca Goldstone, Dennis Stokes, Christine Weddle
9-781-60006-261-2
1-60006-261-X

Receiving God's love and in turn loving others is God's plan for us. But loving others as ourselves is not always easy. Learn how to reach out in love to family, friends, and others who may be more difficult to love.

Life: Thriving in a Complex World

Ralph Ennis, Judy Gomoll, Rebecca Goldstone, Dennis Stokes, Christine Weddle
978-1-60006-260-5
1-60006-260-1

Explore important areas—time, money, decisions, commitment—that play a role in living life well with Jesus.

To order copies, call NavPress at 1-800-366-7788, or log on to www.navpress.com.

NAVPRESS

BE TRANSFORMED

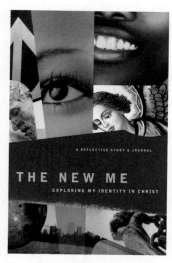